Praise for *Good Self, Bad Self*

"Judy Smith is a very savvy problem solver, and she's incredibly tough. I've seen her handle headstrong clients and also senior producers of major television shows, and in each case, she was in command and relentless in working to implement her strategies. I hope to continue to watch her work her magic from afar, and never to need her services as a client."

—Wayne Pacelle, president and CEO, The Humane
    Society of the United States

"Judy Smith has been doling out practical, no-nonsense advice for over twenty years to her clients and her friends. *Good Self, Bad Self* is Judy in book form. Having worked with Judy and one of her clients over the course of several months, I got to witness her style and effectiveness firsthand. She is detailed, thorough, relentless, frank, and smart. Her course of action while strategic is also very thoughtful and client-sensitive."

—James Brown, network broadcaster, CBS Sports

"Judy Smith is the uber media-management guru of the twenty-first century. In a 24-7 breaking news world of sound bites, there is no better media veteran to have on speed dial than Judy Smith."

—Linda Kenney Baden, high-profile trial attorney, media
    legal commentator, and coauthor of *Remains Silent*
    and *Skeleton Justice*

"Judy Smith and her team are a reference encyclopedia of knowledge combined with experience that can command, guide, handle, influence, instruct, steer, supervise, and take overall charge of media relations with laser-sharp understanding of the complex issues of law, medicine, and forensic science."

—Dr. Michael Baden, host of HBO's hit show *Autopsy*
    and coauthor of *Unnatural Death* and *Dead Reckoning*

fP

Good Self, BAD SELF

TRANSFORMING YOUR WORST QUALITIES INTO YOUR BIGGEST ASSETS

JUDY SMITH

FREE PRESS

NEW YORK   LONDON   TORONTO   SYDNEY   NEW DELHI

NOTE TO READERS

The stories about nonpublic figures in this book are intended to be illustrative. They are composites based on the author's extensive experience as a crisis manager, and they do not depict the experiences of any particular person. In addition, the identifying and other details in some of the author's anecdotes about corporations or individuals are stories that are illustrative and do not represent an actual incident or particular corporation.

*f*P

FREE PRESS
A Division of Simon & Schuster, Inc.
1230 Avenue of the Americas
New York, NY 10020

First Free Press hardcover edition April 2012

FREE PRESS and colophon are trademarks of Simon & Schuster, Inc.

For information about special discounts for bulk purchases, please contact Simon & Schuster Special Sales at 1-866-506-1949 or business@simonandschuster.com

The Simon & Schuster Speakers Bureau can bring authors to your live event. For more information or to book an event contact the Simon & Schuster Speakers Bureau at 1-866-248-3049 or visit our website at www.simonspeakers.com.

Designed by Julie Schroeder

Manufactured in the United States of America

1 3 5 7 9 10 8 6 4 2

Library of Congress Cataloging-in-Publication Data

Smith, Judy.
Good self, bad self : transforming your worst qualities into your biggest assets / by Judy Smith.
p. cm.
1. Change (Psychology) 2. Success. I. Title.
BF637.C4S57 2012
158—dc23
2012002796

ISBN: 978-1-4516-4999-4
ISBN: 978-1-4516-5001-3 (ebook)

For my mother and father—I would not be in this place in life without your love and hard work.

For my sisters and brother—Deborah, Vaughn, Denise, and Tracy—there is so much love in my heart for all of you. Deborah—thanks for taking care of all of us when we could not take care of ourselves. Vaughn—thanks for always being there; I could not ask for a better brother. Denise—I am blessed to have you in my life and am so proud of you. Tracy—you are turning out to be quite a big sister.

To Bill, Austin, and Cody—you have changed my life in ways I could never have imagined. Life brought me the biggest gift with the three of you.

And to all the people who have made mistakes, screwed up, or gotten into trouble, and for those who face a crisis or find themselves in a situation they never anticipated, may you know that there is a way through it and a second act waiting on the other side.

CONTENTS

Good Self,
BAD SELF

INTRODUCTION

My mobile phone woke me at 1:42 a.m. I scrambled for it on the night table. Squinting at the Los Angeles area code, I tapped the talk icon, cleared my throat, and, as always, resisted the temptation to start with "Do you have any idea what time it is?" Instead I answered with my usual cheerful greeting. "This is Judy Smith," I said.

I could sense the panic pulsing through the line; the caller was the CEO of a huge California corporation with a colossal emergency on his hands: He'd just learned that the head of the international arm of one of his companies was being threatened with a giant sexual harassment lawsuit. He wasn't sure exactly what the executive at one of his companies had done, or even if he'd done anything. How should the CEO handle it? What should he do when the press showed up at his door? What the hell was he supposed to say to the stockholders, especially since he didn't yet have all the facts? All the CEO knew was that the repercussions would be serious. He was exactly right. His job, not to mention his reputation and future employability, would all be on the line.

In a half-furious, half-terrified tone, the CEO told me the

meager details he knew so far. As I listened my eyes scanned the room, and I was reminded that I wasn't at home in Washington, D.C. I'd arrived in New York late the night before to meet with a new client, and now I was in an anonymous hotel room in downtown Manhattan.

Still holding the phone to my ear, I padded across the plush carpet to the desk, sat down, flipped open my laptop, and started typing. "How could this happen?" the CEO on the phone kept asking. "How could it have happened on my watch?" He took a deep breath. "And what the hell am I going to do now?"

I've heard variations of these three questions more times than I can count. It's my job to help people figure out how they wound up in the unenviable situation they're in, and how to regroup, fix the problem, and deal with the fallout. As a professional crisis manager, that is what I do for a living, every hour of the day, every day of the year.

My two sons, Austin and Cody, who regularly express astonishment at my inability to follow driving directions (whether issued by a human or a GPS), find it hard to believe that anyone sees their mom as a coolheaded, problem-solving pro. But crisis management is an entirely different kind of navigation, one I'm quite good at. So perhaps it would be more accurate to describe me as an expert at handling other people's crises. News flash for my boys: I am the one to call when the loss of direction belongs to someone else, as long as it's a huge, metaphorical loss of direction.

Now, before you immediately put this book down because you don't believe you have a crisis to manage, or at least not one that's on par with what you're likely to see on tomorrow's morning news, let me be clear: The purpose of this book is to show how my work applies to you and to the entire spectrum of crises we find ourselves in, as well as share a wealth of practical strategies to navigate the world better. Have you ever gotten yourself into a situation you wish you hadn't? Said something you wish you could take back? Done something that's hurt your reputation or your relationships? Made a bad decision that's cost you more than you bargained for? Or simply failed at getting what you want out of life due to too many setbacks and disappointments? If you've said yes to any of these questions, then this book is for you. If you said no, then this book is even more for you.

After a career of more than twenty-five years helping politicos, celebrities, and captains of industry cope with the messy truths in their lives, I'm eager to pass along the lessons I've learned. And here's the crux of it: None of us is perfect. Expecting perfection—in life, work, interpersonal relationships, health habits, driving, studying, you name it—is a surefire ticket to failure.

While you may have already known that deep down, what you might not realize is that our best qualities and our worst traits are actually one and the same. That's why I've titled this book *Good Self, Bad Self.* The secret to living the life you want and staying out of personal crisis is knowing what drives you and being self-aware and self-policing enough to make sure those traits stay positive instead of turning negative. That goes for managing others effectively as well.

That freaked-out CEO on the phone? His management style—letting each division head have a great deal of freedom—encouraged the creativity and flexibility that allowed his many companies to soar, but his lack of direct engagement also led to his cluelessness about the possible bad behavior of one honcho. That's just one example of how what makes people successful in life and in business can be the same trait that gets them into trouble.

I came to this realization over many years. In fact, at age eleven I fixed my first interpersonal disaster, the tragic break-up of the "it" couple of my middle school in Washington, D.C., where I grew up. Let's call them Michele and Lloyd. After the tween rumor mill had done its dirty work, Michele was positive that Lloyd kissed another girl. He steadfastly denied it. I had a reputation as a good listener and problem solver, so Lloyd came to me to plead his case. After hearing his side, I was convinced he was telling the truth. I went to Michele and persuaded her that Lloyd was still her Prince Charming. The magic words I culled from Lloyd's verbal river of desperation? "Judy, why would I want to kiss another girl in school! Only a fool would risk messing that up!" They were so sincere and heartfelt that they struck me as true, and it didn't hurt that it was what Michele wanted to believe about herself. When I repeated his sentiments to Michele, the crisis was over as quickly as it had begun. She declared me her new best friend. I had saved their relationship . . . which lasted another week before they grew bored with each other. Michele and Lloyd were just a teaser of what was to come.

From there I moved on to my first corporate crisis involving a local company, Sam's Print Shop. Sam decided to cut funding for the after-school program held at the playground up the street. The playground director, Francine, sadly told all the parents and kids that softball, ballet, and tap were being eliminated. The uproar was instantaneous. We kids were devastated to lose the activities we loved, as well as the justification we used to get away from our parents until dinnertime. Our parents were traumatized to lose the unofficial neighborhood babysitting service.

I decided to take action. Over the next few days, I helped Francine come up with a plan that included producing flyers, going door-to-door with other kids to enlist neighbors in our cause, and petitioning other businesses to pick up the slack in funding the after-school program. Eventually Sam's kicked in a little money, so did the local dry cleaner, the supermarket, and a few other businesses. With everyone pitching in (and not so coincidentally, getting positive publicity for stepping up to help the kids), we kept the playground program alive. My first taste of grassroots organizing helped me realize that no crisis was insurmountable. And I still believe in that to this day.

The Balancing Act

Of all the lessons and strategies you'll learn in this book, perhaps the biggest one of all is simply this: A little good old-fashioned self-evaluation can keep you from ending up in the unfortunate position of some of the crisis-ridden folks you read about or see on TV. This book isn't just for people in trouble. It's for anyone who wants to find and maintain success in his or her professional and personal life. My goal is to help you think about the elements that might keep you on track in your career and your relationships or help you get back on track if you've gone astray.

My book is for anyone and everyone who finds himself or herself getting in his or her own way. It's for people who want to know how to change the patterns that get them into trouble—sometimes that's a matter of looking forward with authenticity and introspection; sometimes it's a matter of working backward from the desired outcome to the crisis at hand. It's for people who let ego or pride get them into predicaments that feel out of their control, for people who consistently find themselves putting a foot in their mouth, for people who keep denying the truth—and it's even for people who just want to get ahead in life and learn how to harness their inner powers while keeping those same assets in check so they don't become liabilities. It's for those who have a tendency to make bad situations worse inadvertently, or for those who struggle with making situations better.

Although I have rarely found there to be only a single cause for the occurrence of a crisis—or for that matter only one solution—the root causes of most crises often lie in an imbalance in one of seven traits: Ego, Denial, Fear, Ambition, Accommodation, Patience, and Indulgence. All these attributes can be blessings as well as curses; they're positive qualities when you manage them well and usually create a crisis when you don't. The momentum they provide can keep you moving forward in your career and in your life, but out of control they cause you to crash and burn. Some of us have many of these characteristics; some of us have only one or two. In any case, the key to avoiding personal and professional disaster is keeping all these properties in balance.

A Lifelong Career in the Trenches

What qualifies me to give this advice—sans the PhD and MD? I've been on the front lines and behind the scenes, managing myriad types of crises in the real world for decades, so my perspective is hands-on and realistic. I started my career at the Office of the Independent Counsel, where I worked on the Iran-Contra prosecution of Oliver North. Later, I was a prosecutor and Special Assistant at the U.S. Attorney's office in Washingon, D.C., where I worked on high-profile cases, including the prosecution of Mayor Marion Barry for drug possession. In 1991, I was appointed a Special Assistant and Deputy Press Secretary to President George H. W. Bush; in the White House I worked on a huge variety of foreign and domestic issues, including the allegations of sexual harassment made by Anita Hill during Clarence Thomas's Supreme Court nomination hearings. I've worked on the Enron Congressional inquiry, advised Fortune 500 companies, and assisted foreign governments ranging from Haiti to Zimbabwe to Saudi Arabia.

My firm, Smith & Co., sometimes feels a little like the Justice League of America. At any moment, we might receive a call from someone who needs help. At the drop of a hat, I rally the team and we sprint to the next plane.

On the flight, we replay, reassess, and reanalyze that frenzied phone call. We never quite know what we're getting into: How deep does the problem go? Who are all the parties involved? What moves has the person in crisis made in an attempt to evade whatever it is he or she dreads so much? One thing is for sure, there is never a dull moment around here. As we get to know the client, we help him or her craft a strategy and a path for the future. If the client just wants the problem to go away and doesn't want to look at the root causes of his or her predicament, my job is infinitely harder.

Managing scandals and crises may be the most sensational part of what I do, but it's not everything. My team and I have been involved in some of the largest health crises in modern history. When the Severe Acute Respiratory Syndrome (SARS) pandemic swept the country, we helped get vital information to the public and calm the international hysteria. We've advised governmental organizations working on the foreclosure crisis, and helped educate people about housing scams in this time of economic anxiety.

I've also worked with people who never expected to find themselves in the public eye, like Monica Lewinsky and her family, and the family of the tragically murdered young federal intern Chandra Levy. I've been quoted as a crisis expert in publications and on television. As I write this, Shonda Rhimes, the creator of *Grey's Anatomy* and *Private Practice,* and her partner Betsy Beers, are working on a dramatic series for ABC-TV called *Scandal* inspired by my work. Thanks to the miracle of television, I have become the talented Kerry Washington.

Indeed, some of my clients have been controversial fig-ures. Before you rush to judgment on any or all of them, I'd argue that they still deserve a fair hearing and the opportunity to learn from whatever mistakes they've made. I would also point out that as a culture, we love to turn on powerful figures and are ever quick to demonize. The media maw gets bigger every year; we seem to have an insatiable appetite for paparazzi pics, insinuating blog posts, incriminating whispers, and the twenty-four-hour onslaught of disapproving gossip. People are always delighted to find someone new to tear down. We tend to see the world in binary terms—sinner or saint, angel or devil—but I think life is much more nuanced than that. The same traits that make you successful can be your downfall. That's the root of most crises and the point of this book.

I do have my own personal code. There are cases I won't take. It's hard for me to generalize about cases I've turned down—as Supreme Court Justice Potter Stewart said about obscenity: it's difficult to define, but I know it when I see it; it's often a gut call. When something doesn't feel right to me about a case, or the facts, or even what the client may be try-ing to achieve, I will pass.

Nonetheless, I firmly believe that most people who are willing to take responsibility for their own actions and who are repentant deserve a second chance. You deserve that same courtesy. Though we may not want to admit it, there's a "bad guy" inside all of us. We're all flawed in some way. All of us are capable of poor judgment and bad behavior. What can help us in business, life, and love is knowing our failings and being honest about them.

A wonderful quality about America is that we love re-demption stories. We're quick to lash out and assign blame, but we also draw from deep reservoirs of forgiveness. The scope, severity, and impact of the challenge change with the client and situation, but everyone we work with is looking for help and redemption. What I've discovered is that regard-less of stature, power, celebrity, or wealth, crisis is a great lev-eler. Everyone makes mistakes. And the solution to them is often similar regardless of who we are. At some point in time, we'll all need help. That's true whether you're a celebrity or a "real person." I've worked with all kinds of people (and in this book, I'll offer crisis-management case studies from folks who are household names and everyday people whose lives will never make the papers).

A Quick Tour of the Big Seven

I've organized this book by traits, devoting a single chapter to each of the seven chief traits that compose the good self/bad self. I end the book with an appendix dedicated to the art of apology, which you'll learn can be one of the most important elements in preserving your good self, and your reputation.

Before we launch into the first chapter, however, let's take a brief tour of each trait and gain a little perspective on how and why these particular attributes can be so powerfully enriching—and destructive—to each one of us. This will set the tone for the rest of the book, and prepare you to maximize your read-ing experience. Some, such as Ego, Ambition, and Accommodation, are "personality definers," the traits that motivate us to action. The other four, Denial, Fear, Indulgence, and Patience, are more typically responses to the situations we may find ourselves in. These qualities are neither perfect nor imperfect; they just are. Whether they work for you, or against you, is up to you.

The Big Seven

EGO

You need a strong ego to succeed, but it can also be your undoing. On one hand, being modest and unassuming leads to a modest and unassuming life. On the other hand, a rampaging ego can make you lose everything you've gained. Can you listen to input? Can you own your mistakes? What constitutes healthy and unhealthy ego? This chapter will help you answer these questions.

DENIAL

To some degree, you need denial to get anywhere; you have to ignore the fact that the odds are often stacked against success. If Mrs. Fields had acknowledged how difficult it is for a small business to succeed, let alone become a giant company, would she have ever attempted to sell a single chocolate chip cookie? On a personal level, choosing not to focus on your partner's less endearing qualities can help you stay happily married. But denial can also be a hugely destructive quality.

Denying communication problems in a marriage can lead to greater and greater distance. So how do you find a middle ground? How can you make sure denial is an asset instead of a liability, for you?

FEAR

Fear can be galvanizing or paralyzing. We are designed, by evolution, to be attuned to fear; it is a survival mechanism. Fear keeps us alert; the ability to flee danger can keep us safe. But fear can also stop us from taking the risks that could take our lives—romantic, professional, interpersonal—to the next level. Reading this chapter should help you determine whether your fear is holding you back or keeping you on the straight and narrow. I'll also share some research on channeling your fears so that they fuel your success rather than freezing you in your tracks.

AMBITION

Ambition gets you up the ladder of work and life. But excess ambition can mean overreaching (shooting for or taking jobs you're not ready for, or cheating to reach your goal faster), and can destroy your personal life (lack of attention to loved ones). How do we manage ambition so that it gives us the lives we want but doesn't eat everything in its path?

ACCOMMODATION

While it's vital to get along with others, it's also imperative that you not do so at the expense of your own voice and your own dreams. Trying to make everyone happy—spouse, children, parents, friends, boss, colleagues—can ultimately hurt you badly. At work, people sometimes find that being the "go-to guy" means that no one else wants to see you promoted, because you're the perfect doormat right where you are. In the home sphere, being a "good doo-bee," someone who quietly works around other people's damage and avoids confrontation, can be soul crushing. So how can you be the helpful, giving person you want to be, without subverting and shortchanging yourself in the process?

PATIENCE

Being patient is good. Until it isn't. Sometimes bosses are too patient with hires they really want to work out. Sometimes CEOs are too patient with strategies they hope will turn a company around. Sometimes parents are too patient with children who need a real wake-up call. Sometimes we're too patient with people and projects that don't add to our lives and should be dismissed. Meaningful change usually comes incrementally, so how do we set the wheels in motion without going so slowly nothing can be accomplished, or too quickly to give things time to improve? On the flip side, having no patience at all leads to so many missed opportunities: life happens in the pauses.

INDULGENCE

A life without indulgence is no life at all. Parties, cake, fine wine—they can all bring joy and excitement to a quotidian world. But indulgence can become overindulgence all too quickly, hurting our health, relationships, and standing in the community. This chapter can help you recognize whether the pendulum has swung too far in one direction or the other, toward decadence and hedonism on the one side or toward asceticism and self-abnegation on the other. I'll also try to help you think about where your own personal line is.

The P.O.W.E.R. Approach

The ultimate goal of understanding how these seven traits operate in your own life is to ensure that your defining traits work to your advantage instead of your detriment.

So here's the big question: Knowing that we all have qualities that can swing either way, for us or against us, how do we make sure they're working in our service? The answer is in making sure we maintain balance. That's why I've created a mnemonic device called the POWER approach.

I've always liked mnemonic devices. They're a simple formula that can help you pull back from the drama and assess, which is really at the core of crisis management. When it comes to looking at positive traits that can spin out into negativity, I use the mnemonic reminder: POWER. You have the power to stop and regain your balance when your traits are pushing you out of a state of equilibrium and control. Here's how:

Pinpoint the core trait: Identify which trait is in play.
Own it: Acknowledge that it can be both good and bad.
Work it through: Process the role it's played in your life.
Explore it: Consider how it could play out in the future.
Rein it in: Establish how to re-achieve balance and control.

In each chapter, we'll examine the POWER approach in action. Once you learn how these factors work and can apply the POWER model, you'll have the ability to manage problems or even avoid them in the first place. I'll help you identify the way certain character pluses can turn into minuses—and most of the time, if you're honest with yourself, you'll actually learn to see disaster looming, take steps to minimize or prevent it, and keep your life on track. I'll also give you questions and issues to think about to further ascertain whether you're keeping those seven essential qualities in balance.

If you're already in the midst of a crisis (perhaps that's why you picked up this book) . . . well, I'll help you ride it out. The upside of crisis is the opportunity to take a good look at yourself, and confront and then resolve the challenges that have held you back. With self-reflection and a willingness to change direction, you free yourself to move on and pursue what's really important to you.

1

EGO

NEEDING TO BE THE SMARTEST
PERSON IN THE ROOM

He was considered a brilliant attorney: charismatic, good-looking, and with one of the best conviction rates in any major metropolitan area. He was considered a shoo-in to be the next State Attorney General and he was being groomed for much more, Governor, Senator, maybe even President. At least to hear him tell it. "You know what it is, Judy? Truthfully, a lot of people are jealous of my success. Did you know that I'll be the youngest State Attorney General in history?" You haven't been elected yet, I thought to myself, although I'm sure as far as he was concerned that was just a formality. He had no problem with confidence, which, along with his other assets, made him attractive to the public. Yet he had run into a glitch; he was being accused of having withheld evidence in a trial he received a lot of publicity for winning. "It's absurd. With my conviction rate why would I need to cheat?" I could see that I would have to craft his media responses for him and insist that he adhere to them, but it was

going to be an uphill battle because I could tell he thought he was
always the smartest person in the room.

———

When people talk about someone who has an ego, it's almost never meant as a compliment; it's a three-letter dirty
word, used interchangeably with "arrogance" or "pompos-
ity," and the word "big" usually precedes it. But ego isn't
inherently bad or good. It's merely one quality among many
that make up a human being. Back in the day, of course,
Freud used the word to talk about the conscious mind—our
amazing human ability to impose control on our wild id.
Now, though, the word has fallen out of favor with psychia-
trists, precisely because it means so many different things to
different people.

We're not looking at it in the Freudian sense, but rather
how most of us use it colloquially. In this chapter, we'll take
a look at ego in both its positive and negative sense. Indeed,
having a healthy ego is essential to a happy, successful life, and
like the other aspects of the self we discuss in this book, you
have to own the quality and make it work for you instead of
against you.

First off, what's good about having a healthy ego? Many,
many things. A strong sense of self is essential to accomplish-
ing anything in this world. Ego gives us that. We need to like
ourselves, to think that we're deserving of attention and our
opinions and ideas are worthy of consideration. That isn't arrogance; it's the key to emotional health. "This is not a brag-
ging or self-assertive liking," wrote Carl Rogers, one of the

founders of humanistic psychology, in 1961's *On Becoming a Person*. "It is a quiet pleasure in being one's self."

Embracing your healthy ego doesn't mean being a domineering jerk or spending your days trying to make the world fit into an overblown conception of who you are. A strong ego can confer confidence, independence, leadership, as well as the strength to buck conventional wisdom and stand up for what you believe. A powerful sense of self can help you lead and give you the passion to sell your vision to others. Our country was built on the values of self-reliance, confidence, drive, and bootstrapping your way to success, and there's no question that the men and women who founded it had generous egos under their powdered wigs. But there is a fine line between encouraging a strong sense of self with high expectations and creating an atmosphere of arrogance and self-importance. It is important that aiming high does not turn into stomping on others on your way to the top. Arrogance is not an admirable quality. We've all encountered self-promoters who are eager to tell us how fantastic they are rather than let us figure that out by ourselves—this is just one example of how off-putting it can be when ego is used for ill rather than for good.

The balance that keeps someone with a healthy sense of self from becoming a self-involved, egocentric person is tipped when the ambitions of the self run roughshod over the needs of others. Because when the ego rampages unchecked, it stomps on good judgment, self-analysis, and self-control. An ego without limits is like a car with no brakes; if you can't figure out how to regain control, you may well wind up driving right off a cliff. This chapter is about finding your own point of balance and making sure that your ego is a reliable copilot and not a carjacker taking you for a ride.

In this chapter, we'll talk about different ways ego manifests and how it can get the best of you. We'll look at entitlement; engaging in risky, provocative behavior; having a sense of self that depends on external validation; failing to consider the consequences of one's actions; and refusing to admit you've made a mistake—all of which allow your ego to blind you to the landscape you inhabit. These are all both evidence and consequence of an ego run wild, and it's easy to see how someone who is unaware of the effects of his ego can get embroiled in a crisis that feels impossible to get out of. This chapter is about finding the line between being motivated by ego and being consumed by it. If you can begin to recognize when your ego is taking over in a negative way and check it, you'll be able to channel the positive aspects of ego—those that lead to business accomplishments, ethical leadership, and healthy relationships—to your benefit.

Ego Run Amok
As a crisis manager, I unfortunately tend to get called in when the balance between the good and bad aspects of someone's ego has already shifted way out of whack. I've heard celebrities wailing about the unfairness of the universe more times than I care to count—even when it's clear to everyone around them that they alone are responsible for their downfall. To get out of their situations (or at least control the dam-

age) they sometimes need to realize the problem is internal, as well as external. That can be a terribly difficult concept for egocentric people to wrap their minds around.

Take Kanye West, for example. The man is a brilliant hip-hop artist, but most of his public missteps appear to stem from an inflated ego and a refusal to see his own role in each debacle. I hardly need to list the flubs: from his televised declaration during the benefit for Hurricane Katrina relief that "George Bush doesn't care about black people," to his comparing himself to Jesus Christ, to his predilection for awards-show outbursts—most notably cutting off the very young Taylor Swift at the 2009 MTV Video Music Awards to say that Beyoncé should have won the award that Swift was in the middle of accepting. Even President Obama called him a "jackass." West's arrogance isn't just cringe-worthy for those of us who watch him make similar mistakes again and again. It also affects his public image.

West, of course, is driven by passionate emotions, which is okay (necessary, even) for an artist whose job it is to express thoughts and feelings that we all can recognize. The recording studio is the ideal place for his ego to receive full expression, a forum for all his ideas and emotions that would serve to make his music even more affecting. But when he's not in the studio, West sometimes appears to fail to analyze those emotions fully before they come flying out of his mouth, and context does matter. Everyone, from artists who are paid handsomely, precisely because of the way the expression of their emotions touches others, to parents whose ability to teach their children relies on appealing to their kids' emotions at specific moments in their development, needs to remember that no one wants to see or hear you unfiltered all the time.

To me, the first step in reining in an ego that has run amok is taking an accurate read of your own emotions and their intensity; when you feel a burst of anger or aggression coming on, pause to consider those feelings. Often a strong emotional response is a sign that your ego is dominating rather than your objectivity. In West's case, his strong emotional response at the show was a sign that his ego was caught up in the circumstances. So take a deep breath. You don't have to respond to a perceived provocation right away. You cannot accurately make a rational assessment and come to a solid decision if you are acting from a place of unexamined, uncontrolled feeling.

There are two things you can do when you have an intense emotional response and suspect that your ego may be out of balance. First: Wait. Taking that deep breath will give you some time until your feelings are tempered. Second: Write an old-fashioned list of pros and cons for the possible responses you are considering. I am a big fan of lists. This will help you determine exactly what you are trying to accomplish by taking a particular course of action, and in the time it takes to write the list, your emotions will calm down, allowing your rational side to emerge. And if there are hidden egotistical motivations involved, you'll soon uncover them.

West's charging onstage wasn't really about his need to defend Beyoncé's art (and she certainly wasn't asking for his intervention!). It seemed more about West's need to declare himself the arbiter of taste, his need for his voice to be heard above all others that night, heedless of the context. Who won the award, of course, was not his decision to make. Many ego-driven people feel that no matter how they behave, they're going to remain at the top of the heap through their own brilliance, cleverness, and indispensability.

Signs That You Need an Ego Check

It's not hard to recognize someone who believes he's above it all, is the center of the universe, or is obviously entitled. The stereotypical diva who swoops into a room with demands, expectations, and little patience for anything that doesn't immediately support her view of herself as central to the universe is an obvious example of someone whose ego is off the charts. But most people with an ego problem don't present that way. While not subtle, there are some less overt traits and behaviors I've noticed in my years of crisis management that are not thought of as being a sign that ego is running the show. They should be. Recognizing that the root of certain behaviors is an ego run amok is the only way to get back in a more productive ego balance.

Ego-driven Tendency 1: Displaying an Overblown Sense of Entitlement

Entitlement is the overriding sense that you deserve certain things in life, regardless of whether you've earned them. I've come to believe that certain types of people are prone to egocentrism, and with it, an outsize concept of what they are entitled to. You would probably not be shocked to learn that a recent study by *Celebrity Rehab* host Dr. Drew Pinsky found that celebrities are significantly more narcissistic than the general population, after he had a sample of two hundred celebrities complete the Narcissistic Personality Inventory, a test measuring self-absorption. What's interesting is that the celebrities who had a talent (for example, musicians) tended to be less narcissistic than folks who were famous for simply being famous.

This squares with other research and my own experience: If you're good at something and have worked at it, as opposed to getting acclaim for something you didn't earn (inherited wealth, position, beauty, or having grown up with overindulgent parents), you're less inclined to feel like a fake. Persevering to get where you are (in the case of a musician, playing in small clubs and dusty dives, gradually honing your art and paying your dues) makes you more likely to have a manageable ego than someone who has catapulted to prominence without developing meaningful skills.

I will always thank my parents for conveying to me that working hard is essential. My parents taught me to treat everyone the same: with respect. My mom was an administrative assistant who cleaned office buildings at night. Once when I was little she took me to work with her; I was annoyed and a little embarrassed that my mom was the one pushing the vacuum cleaner. She told me firmly, "There is no work you should not be proud of. If you're earning an honest living and doing it well, there is no shame in any kind of work you do." Thanks to their influence, I've never let my head get too swollen as my business has grown. I don't feel entitled to my success. I had to earn it. I think I have a healthy ego about my work—I'm aware that I'm very good at what I do, but I'm also aware that I could lose it all if I don't keep my head on straight.

Ego-driven Tendency 2: Foolishly Taking Risks

When you lose perspective, as ego-imbalanced people tend to, you forget that everything you've worked for can disappear in the blink of an eye. That's what happened to a certain someone who wasn't my client, Congressman Anthony Weiner.

Weiner was hugely popular among his constituents—he won seven terms and more than 58 percent of the vote every time. At twenty-seven, he'd been the youngest city councilman in New York City's history. The ego that gave him confidence and allowed him to make a bid for office at such a young age (and defeat far better-known candidates) is the same ego that fueled his fiery, flamboyant demeanor and caused him to lose perspective.

As you would have to have been in a coma not to know, Weiner tweeted photos of himself in his underwear to at least one young woman. He was supposedly happily married, with a baby on the way. Nonetheless, Weiner had text or phone dalliances with at least five other women. Before owning up to the truth, he spent a week bobbing and weaving while late-night comedians had a field day at his expense (it didn't help that his name is slang for the very part of his anatomy he photographed and then tweeted). Finally, when his reputation was thoroughly tarnished, he held a tearful press conference during which he owned up to sending the pictures. He admitted that it was "a very dumb thing to do" and added, "But if you are looking for some sort of deep explanation for it I don't have one for you."

Well, I do, at least in part. Some of us are simply hard-wired to get off on risky behavior. Brian Knutson, a neuro-scientist at Stanford, conducted a study in 2005 in which he put Wall Street traders into MRI machines. Then he scanned their brains as they evaluated whether to buy or sell certain stocks. The higher the risk entailed in the decisions the traders needed to make, the more activity was visible in the pleasure centers of their brains on the MRI. I believe that part of the appeal for people who are attracted to high-risk professions like gambling, trading stocks, or politics is feeling as though they're superior to the people who aren't taking the bold chances, that they know more and can juggle more. That leads to a certain sense that you are not subject to the same pitfalls as others, or that you are so good you will not get caught.

That is really a form of ego. Politics itself is a risky business, and you need a certain amount of healthy ego to believe you can serve others, put yourself out there, and get elected. Weiner's ego took an unhealthy turn when it drove him toward the risky thrill of tweeting dirty pictures. The problem was that this same too-healthy ego blinded him to the fact that he would inevitably get caught and would lose everything as a result. He thought himself above risk (a form of denial we discuss in the next chapter). And losing everything is exactly what ended up happening.

Ego-driven Tendency 3: Doing Anything to Be Validated

"Fragile high self-esteem" is what social scientists call the need for perpetual validation and praise in order for someone's sense of self to remain intact. The person appears to have a healthy ego, but it's an illusion. Without positive feedback, his sense of self flounders. People with fragile high self-esteem need affirmation all the time because despite their bluster, they actually aren't as secure as they seem. They can't afford to be wrong—they can't afford to even admit the possibility of being wrong—because that would pop their puffed-up sense of self.

It's not surprising that the insecurity found in those with fragile high self-esteem is correlated with lower psychological well-being and more defensiveness, as Brian Goldman, a professor of psychology at Clayton State University, has found. People with "secure high self-esteem," however—which is what I'm calling an ego in balance—are genuinely confident in who they are and value their strengths, but also understand and learn to adjust to their weaknesses. Because they are not invested in being perceived as having it all together, they don't need to be defensive or act out as much when that premise is challenged. In short, if you have an in-balance ego, although it is still nice to hear it sometimes, you don't strictly *need* outsiders to keep telling you how fantastic you are in order to feel good about yourself. You've internalized that you're a good person doing a good job.

Being dependent on the praise of others is a very precarious way to live, and I see that in some of my work. The risks of relying on the affirmation of others are quite high, especially if you're a performer or politician, because if you fall out of favor (and most do at some point or another) and your acolytes trot off to find someone else to fawn over, you have no solid foundation to fall back on. Some people spend an inordinate amount of time and effort cultivating people to tell them how attractive and brilliant they are. A person with secure self-esteem needn't do this, and is not likely to throw all the good things in his life away (whether over time or in a single tweet) in the pursuit of external praise.

We see this all the time in parents. Parents with fragile high self-esteem often seek ego gratification through their kids, feeding off the praise and achievements of their offspring. It's seen in soccer moms or dads who are more competitive and invested in the game than their children are, or people who feel where their children attend school is a reflection of their worth as parents.

Here's one example: Despite doing well in school and in her career, Serena always felt a little intimidated by people who'd attended Ivy League schools. It didn't dominate her life, but after she married and had children, this insecurity, which had been dormant, was reawakened. Serena secretly decided when her kids were only infants that she wanted them to go to Ivy League schools.

Indeed, when her oldest was in high school, she began insisting that schools in the Midwest, where they lived, weren't up to par. Despite the fact that her son really liked Carleton, Grinnell, and Macalester—superb small schools not far from home—Serena kept pushing him to apply to the Ivies. She believed with all her heart that it was about setting Henry up for success in the world and that he would thrive at Princeton or University of Pennsylvania or Cornell. The fact that Henry wanted a small college instead of a large university, and the fact that he wanted to be close to his family and high school friends in Chicago, didn't seem to matter to Serena.

Serena pushed him and nagged him about it to the extent that he felt alienated from her, and was even less likely to consider her point of view. He sensed that her desire for him to go to an Ivy didn't have to do with him. When he decided to go to Grinnell, which is in Iowa, over the one Ivy League school he got into, she was crushed and experienced it as a personal slight—if he loved and respected her, she reasoned, he wouldn't have "done that" to her. They didn't speak for his senior year of high school and well into his freshman year of college, which was painful for them both.

Parents like Serena don't truly see the distinction between themselves and their offspring, pushing the kids to excel in part because it's a reflection on them. They aren't truly interested in their children's interests or needs; they just need the affirmation of having other people be impressed by their kids' accomplishments. Her blindness to what her ego was doing to her outlook and opinions made her feel anxious and powerless.

Maybe you're not the kind of parent who's obsessed with

the "right" school . . . but have you ever pushed your children into a sport or performing art that you once participated in—because you were just sure they'd love it once they gave it a chance, even if they weren't naturally inclined to try it? Do you want your child to have friends from socially prominent or attractive families mainly because you feel that his associations will reflect well on you? Any pursuit in which a parent lives through his or her kid tends to be an unhealthy instance of egotism. Recognizing this can save you, and your child, years of misery and/or therapy bills.

Ego-driven Tendency 4: Overreacting and Catastrophizing

Another manifestation of ego is overreacting. The ego can be a frail thing indeed and people with a massive ego tend to protect and defend it at all costs. Excessive ego fuels emotional states that are prone to overreaction.

The London-born supermodel Naomi Campbell is notorious for her "world revolves around me" attitude. It probably doesn't hurt to have a healthy dose of ego when you work in an industry that constantly judges and critiques your physical appearance and demands adherence to its ideals of "perfection." But a healthy balance of ego is perhaps a description that has never been applied to Campbell. Her emotional responses to confrontation and dissatisfaction in her life most likely stem from a warped perspective caused by an inflated self-importance.

People with inflated self-importance will tend to view every circumstance, frustration, or dispute as a personal affront to their identity, which needs to be defended—sometimes even in violent ways. Furthermore, because their self-importance makes them feel threatened and more vulnerable, egomaniacs will often view themselves as victims by unrealistically inflating the importance of neutral comments and occurrences—oftentimes finding nefarious meanings that aren't there, or tying a random event's origin back to themselves.

In 2006, Naomi Campbell was involved in a highly publicized scandal in which she was arrested for second-degree assault against her maid. The housekeeper alleged that Campbell accused her of stealing a missing pair of jeans . . . and then threw a cell phone at her, hitting her on the head. Campbell initially pleaded not guilty to the charges and claimed that she believed that the maid was retaliating for being fired earlier that day. But this was not the first time Campbell had been accused of assault using this MO.

Back in 2003, Campbell was sued by a former assistant who alleged that two years earlier, the supermodel had assaulted her during a fit of rage. She accused Campbell of throwing a cell phone at her in a Beverly Hills hotel. According to various news publications, the assistant claimed that she was grabbed by the arms and thrown down on the couch. Media outlets also reported, in a separate incident, in February 2000, that Campbell pleaded guilty in Toronto to assaulting her assistant over the course of several days in 1998.

Ironically, even when a reaction is spurred by a warped

perspective, where people feel justified in their behavior, such as thinking they have been wronged in some way, they often have trouble accepting responsibility (notice how denial and ego align themselves in fueling crisis situations). Instead of saying "l was wrong," which would threaten their ego, they often place blame on anything or anyone else. They also are quick to tie unrelated events together and assign meaning to them. Consider Campbell's statement, issued by her spokesman, regarding her 2006 cell-phone tirade reported on *People* magazine's website: "We believe [the charge] is a case of retaliation, because Naomi had fired her housekeeper earlier this morning. We are confident the courts will see it the same way."

The court didn't exactly see it the same way. There is no doubt that celebrities are often targeted with litigious threats by those who want to strike it rich using the court of law. But the public (including myself) gave a collective eye roll at Campbell's attempt to downplay her role and minimize responsibility for her actions. In the end, in exchange for a guilty plea, Campbell was ordered to pay her maid's medical fees. She was also sentenced to five days of community service and ordered to attend an anger management program.

Like many with an out-of-whack ego, Campbell also seemed somewhat confused as to who was the real victim. After her 2006 arrest, instead of publicly showing concern for the person who required medical attention because of her outburst, she made sure to assuage the fears that people surely had for her well-being by coyly stating to the press that she was being treated fairly by the police. According to *People* magazine, after her arrest, Campbell told reporters, "I'm fine. The police have been very nice. It wouldn't be the first time I've been extorted." I'm sure the public greeted those words with sympathy and relief.

This would not be the last time Campell would face legal repercussions for her actions.

In 2008. Campbell pleaded guilty to assaulting two police officers at London's Heathrow Airport. She allegedly spat at the officers following an argument about her lost luggage. I can attest to the frustration of being separated from your luggage, especially if it is at the fault of an airline, but a reaction to the circumstance should not result in arrest. *USA Today* reported that Campbell was charged with "three counts of assaulting a constable, two counts of using threatening, abusive words or behavior to the cabin crew and one count of disorderly conduct." Media outlets reported that she has been banned for life from British Airways for her behavior. She was eventually sentenced to 200 hours of community service and fined $4,500 after pleading guilty to assault.

It should be noted that Ms. Campbell, once the dust settled, would often issue apologies for her actions. Her apologies may have rung hollow to more cynical types, though, considering that some sources say that the model had been accused of assault ten times over the course of a decade. Then too, even though she apparently feels "regret" and "shame" for her outbursts, she is often quick to attribute her actions to extenuating circumstances. Regarding the 2006 incident, as reported in *USA Today,* the cause was in part due to "tiredness, lack of sleep (and) just so many things"—all of which caused her to, again, throw a cell phone at another human being in a fit of rage. Also, it was reported in the same publication that "[she] threw a cell phone in the apartment. The cell phone hit [the maid] . . . [but] this was an accident because [she] did not intend to hit her." However, by 2010, Campbell's ego appeared a bit deflated and she seemed to make a more sincere and honest appraisal of her actions. Appearing on *The Oprah Winfrey Show,* an emotional Campbell spoke of her history of violent outbursts: "I am ashamed of everything I've ever done. I take responsibility for the things that I have done, and I do feel a great sense of shame." She continued, "I feel remorseful. I feel ashamed. I feel for them," she said. "[I think,] 'What have I done to them?' If I've hurt them."

Another way that egotists overreact and lose perspective is by ricocheting from perceived disaster to perceived disaster, perpetually in crisis and perpetually dragging others into their drama. Not only is this a waste of energy, but when everyone around you is caught up in the drama, others tend to share your perspective, not challenge it, which makes it harder to right yourself again. When someone turns a setback into a major disaster in his or her mind, therapists call this "catastrophizing." To me, both over- and underestimating the personal impact of a setback are evidence of an ego-driven lack of perspective.

Here's an example of a catastrophist in action. I know a woman named Yvette. If Yvette's kid gets a B, she's positive he'll never get into college. If she misplaces her wallet, the entire criminal underworld is probably charging up the credit cards. If she's having trouble on a project at work, she's certain she's going to get fired and wind up living in a refrigerator box. It seems that much of her distress is about pulling people into her own orbit, gaining sympathy and attention. She doesn't do it consciously; she's a lovely, funny person. She is just a drama queen, convinced that disaster is near.

If you are prone to overreaction, either because you want to appear to be important, or because you need to draw others into your orbit like Yvette, the first thing to do is recognize your pattern. Before you react, consider writing your thoughts down. Writing things down is a great way to gain perspective on them. Over a couple of weeks, you'll start to see what situations lead to your panicking the most, which should help you to avoid them. Then ask yourself what your entrenched behavior is costing you.

If you remember that your ego is only one aspect of you and not in charge, you can "talk back" to your ego-controlling self: Am I really going to be fired because of one mistake in a spreadsheet? Am I really going to go bankrupt because my dishwasher broke? If I come down with an iron fist to solve a problem, might I be causing more harm than good? Then answer yourself honestly. You can't gain perspective without conscious effort and awareness. But if you make the effort, you'll find that the self-subverting behavior will lessen in strength and frequency.

Ego-driven Tendency 5. Failing to Own the Mistake

People with big egos, in order to preserve that elevated sense of self, are often likely to avoid owning up to their errors, which compounds the problem and creates multilayered crises that can be hard to climb out of. A healthy ego can acknowledge a mistake. Problems with ego often arise when the person with the huge ego happens to be wrong, and stubbornly clinging to the same way of doing things in the face of evidence that it isn't working.

Happily, there are some examples in which a crisis resulting from an out-of-control ego or ego-driven decisions can be turned around. Look at Starbucks. Its leader Howard Schultz exhibited vision and hubris—both sides of the ego coin—with his continual drive toward expansion and disregard for costs and conventional wisdom. The company started in 1971 with six coffee shops in Seattle, then grew to 677 stores in 1995 and 3,505 in 2000, when Schultz left his position as CEO. But the expansion was happening too fast: Stores were dirty and poorly staffed, and consumers in Starbucks-saturated neighborhoods saw the company's name as a synonym for corporate soullessness ruining the character of neighborhoods and snuffing out unionizing and small businesses. The company's stock dropped almost 43 percent in 2007 alone.

In 2008, Schultz decided to return and take the reins again. To his credit, he was not so ego-driven that he couldn't recognize a mistake—that the business model he'd spearheaded was no longer working. In the eighteen months after he took the helm for the second time, Schultz closed hundreds of stores. He also announced that he would take a pay cut from over a million dollars a year to below $10,000 in 2009. Schultz told CNBC's Maria Bartiromo that Starbucks would "go back to our roots and reaffirm our leadership position as the world's highest-quality purveyor of specialty coffee. . . . It reminds me of the old days when our company was very creative, very entrepreneurial, and we were fighting for survival and respect." The company initiated programs to become more environmentally friendly and began opening unbranded coffee- and teahouses in Seattle. The overall financial tides of the company began to turn. Schultz recognized that arrogance had driven the company off course and realized that it was essential to acknowledge their mistakes.

The earlier you recognize and own a mistake, the smaller your crisis will be. In the wonderful book *Mistakes Were Made (but Not by Me)*, the social psychologists Carol Tavris and Elliot Aronson point out, "If you can admit a mistake when it is the size of an acorn, it is easier to repair than when it has become the size of a tree, with deep wide-ranging roots." Shultz and the Starbucks example shows that far from it being a sign of weakness to admit your strategy has its faults, it can be a strength, and yield positive results on a public relations and financial level.

The Role of Perspective in Managing Ego
It's often been said that celebrities live in their own little bubbles, surrounded by people who live off of their earnings and who insulate them from the world. This isolation, combined with a big, potentially problematic ego, which as we've seen can be isolating in itself, can lead to complete loss of perspective. And often perspective from others who aren't invested in the same outcome you are is the only thing that can get an

ego gone wild to calm down. This is just as true of people in positions of power in the workplace.

I call gaining this perspective "knowing your landscape." I find that people who find themselves in ego crises have a far more favorable reading of the landscape than they should, meaning they think that things aren't as bad as they actually are. Knowing the landscape means understanding what you're up against. It means being attuned to the facts, the circumstances, the players involved, and knowing how the issue is perceived by everyone involved, not simply adhering to your point of view in the face of constant opposition. An ego out of control can be incredibly isolating, because inherent in the problem is the belief that you are right, which makes you less likely to seek out the perspective of others. It can also lead to major crisis.

Bill, an executive in a small investment firm, was a boss who was all too eager to throw his employees under the bus every time there was a slip-up, delay, or setback. He was well-known for calling out underperforming underlings in business meetings and shaming them in front of their peers. If he thought an idea was bad, he mocked it roundly, which tended to stifle innovation and creativity. If a client had a complaint, he blamed specific workers or tried to bully the client into agreeing that the complaint was unfounded.

While Bill was at the top of the heap, he won his employees' deference, but only because he was the guy in power. What he didn't have was their respect. When his company was acquired by a larger one, Bill was pushed out. Because he couldn't find anyone with anything truly nice to say about him, he had a hard time getting references. He called me hoping I could help him get his job back; I had to let him know that was impossible. Instead, I tried to help him see how ego—and his refusal to own it and manage it—had torpedoed his hopes.

There's plenty of research to show that ego is a hugely damaging force in the workplace; whether it manifests as a coworker who takes more credit than is due to him or her, an office mate who talks too much (while contributing little of substance) at meetings, or a boss who doesn't value his or her employees, there seems to be no shortage of excessive ego displays at work, particularly among management. A 2009 survey of over 1,200 employees by Florida State University College of Business professor Wayne Hochwarter found that 31 percent of participants reported that their superior exaggerated his or her accomplishments to look good in front of others, 27 percent reported that their boss bragged to others to get praise, 25 percent reported that their boss or the person in charge had an inflated view of himself or herself, 24 percent reported that their boss was self-centered, and 20 percent reported that their boss would do a favor only if guaranteed one in return. "Having a narcissistic boss creates a toxic environment for virtually everyone who must come in contact with this individual," Hochwarter says. "The team perspective ceases to exist, and the work environment becomes increasingly stressful. Productivity typically plummets as well."

Nobody sets out to be an egocentric boss, of course. Bill certainly didn't. As I often do, I took a tough-love approach with Bill. After he filled me in on what happened from his perspective (he felt that people had thrown him under the bus for political reasons) I asked him pointed questions that revealed what had truly taken place with his subordinates. He wasn't completely clueless about his manner. In fact, he took pride in the way he took people to task in public, believing it to be motivational and character building.

I walked him through times in the past when he could have been more of a team player and a more supportive boss, and accomplished similar ends. I encouraged him to speak to a job counselor and a therapist to see how his behavior was harming him professionally and personally. I encouraged him to call some of his former co-workers with whom he'd clashed the least (those who truly hated him were a lost cause; I'm all about looking forward, not backward) and tell them he was sorry for the excesses of his behavior. If he could be specific about ways he'd wronged them, so much the better. Targeted, thoughtful regrets are always better than generalities. I had him spread the word through his network that he was job-hunting and urged him repeatedly to be humble. If he came off as unappreciative or disgruntled, he'd hurt his job-hunting chances still more. He had to show his colleagues—and put the word out into the grapevine—that he was willing to change.

Bill was truly roiled—not to mention deeply embarrassed—by being booted from the company where he'd been a hotshot for so long. But he was willing to do the work of change. It would have been unrealistic to expect an ego-driven guy like Bill to do a complete turnaround, even from a crisis as big as this one, but he was willing to do what he could to repair his reputation and gain employment again. What's more, being humbled actually had a positive impact on his family relationships. A crisis became an opportunity for meaningful change.

Here are some of the questions I had suggested that Bill consider about how large a role his negative ego played in the outcome of his situation; you too might ask them yourself, wherever you fall in the workplace food chain.

> In meetings, what percentage of the time are you the one doing the talking?
>
> Do you give credit for others' ideas?
>
> Do you give other people's contributions and concepts a fair shake, or are you only half listening, looking for evidence that your way of doing things is the best?
>
> When someone comes to you with a problem, is your first reaction "How can we fix this?" or "Who is responsible for this?"

These behaviors are all manifestations of the negative aspects of ego.

If answering those questions sets off your warning bells—and it's OK if they do, because it means you're reading this book openly and with honesty about yourself—here are some steps to try to help get your ego back in check before you reach the point Bill did:

First, recognize the benefit of change. Your work life (and quite possibly other areas of your life) will improve if you take action. If you don't internalize that and truly accept that change is necessary, any change or efforts you make will be purely cosmetic and you'll be prone to backsliding.

Ask for and respond to feedback—that's the perspective component. For example, if you know you tend to talk over everyone else, ask a trusted colleague to help you listen better and integrate the ideas of others.

Think about the example that you're setting. If you're about to demand something nearly impossible, think through how the work will actually get done. Reconsider whether that is the best way to inspire your team. A good way might be to ask *them* what it will take to get what you want done and let them help to set the deadline, so they will be invested in the project, as well as to make yourself available to supervise, not just to expect results.

Make it a point to be empathetic. If you're about to make a snarky public comment about someone's shoddy work, visualize being on the receiving end. You might be correct that the person's work is shoddy. Where someone with an overblown ego is often incorrect, though, is in thinking that any manner in which this fact is pointed out is valuable. It is not. The way in which a criticism is delivered can make the difference between effecting the change you want and simply coming off as mean. Take a minute to think about the best way to improve the quality of the person's work.

Finally, give yourself marks and guideposts and stand by them. For instance, if you tend to dominate meetings, promise yourself you won't speak for the first ten minutes of every meeting. Or vow to ask three information-gathering questions before offering your opinion.

Getting Ego Back into Balance: Reassess, Reevaluate, and Know the Endgame

Getting your ego back in balance is no small feat. In most cases it requires you to step away from the situation, reevaluate, reassess, and really figure out what your endgame is going to look like.

Tiger Woods is a good example of someone who underwent this process. As you no doubt recall, in 2009 Woods was involved in a late-night accident right outside his Florida mansion. The window of his brand-new Cadillac Escalade was smashed. Some speculated that his wife, the former model Elin Nordegren, had used one of her husband's clubs to smash it.

Eventually the story came out that Woods had been unfaithful. Serially. Now, we are accustomed to allegations of bad behavior (often denied) from players in more rough-and-tumble sports—soccer's David Beckham, hockey's Sean Avery, basketball's Tony Parker—but not from a golfer. The sport tends to be very conservative. Tiger's endorsement empire was based on his being above reproach. When he trashed that image, he put at risk everything he had.

So the first thing he did was acknowledge that he had screwed up. He offered a highly orchestrated public apology to an audience of friends, family (though his wife was notably absent), and sympathetic journalists. I thought this was good, in that it was starkly lacking in ego and took full responsibility for having let his fans and family down. And he took a long-term view of making amends: A year after the scandal, Woods made it clear that he was still working toward recovery and self-improvement. In another apology in *Newsweek* he wrote:

Last November, everything I thought I knew about myself changed abruptly. I had been conducting my personal life in an artificial way—as if detached from the values my upbringing had taught, and that I should have embraced. . . . But this much is obvious now: my life was out of balance, and my priorities were out of order. I made terrible choices and repeated mistakes. I hurt the people whom I loved the most.

That's a very wise self-assessment. Woods pointed out that golf was a game that rewarded the individual. It's not a team sport—to an extent, it's about ego and believing that you and only you are the best—and he'd made the mistake of confusing life with golf. He seemed to understand intuitively what I'm saying in this book: the very same qualities that can make you a hero can also make you a villain. The individualism of golf suited Woods; he excelled at a game in which you can't rely on others. But those very same traits of self-focus and raw egocentrism that made him successful at golf suited him poorly in his marriage.

What can you learn from this? That taking a step back is sometimes better than continuing to fight; that in a crisis, you need to figure out what you value and let everything else take a backseat. To Woods, the most important things were family and golf. He tried, and failed, to preserve his marriage but at least felt that the scandal put him on course to be a far better father.

Know your objective and the endgame whenever you hit a snag in your own life. What is it you cherish and fear losing the most? Where do you want to end up? What do you want the most? Do you understand that societal, legal, and moral rules apply to you as much as they do to others? Think of what you need to do and then trace the steps to getting there: don't just react to the crisis in front of you. Think long term.

After all of those examples, it's now time to think more directly about how you can make sure that your own ego is in balance, using the POWER model.

Applying the POWER Model

Pinpoint the core trait: In this case, egotism.
Own it: Acknowledge that it can be both good and bad.
Work it through: Process the role it's played in your life.
Explore it: Consider how it could play out in the future.
Rein it in: Establish how to re-achieve balance and control.

PINPOINT: Take a good, hard look at egotism in your life.

OWN IT: When you own it, you embrace the fact that without ego, you'd be sitting quietly in the corner like a dishrag. You'd never take risks, stand up for yourself, or feel pride in your accomplishments.

WORK IT THROUGH: When you work through your feelings about ego, you'll realize that if you're afraid to ask for what you want, accept and promote your own work and desires, or put your own goals at the top of your agenda, you aren't permitting your ego to help you become the person you could be. But if your ego has become hubris, and you're using ego to domineer and demean, then you're not letting your ego help you become the person you should be.

EXPLORE IT: If your ego isn't in balance, whether that means you have too much or too little, you'll benefit from greater self-analysis (perhaps with the help of a good therapist or friend who is a great listener) to figure out how to make your ego work for you. Who can you engage as an ally in your quest to be your best self? How can you make it up to yourself if you've been shortchanging yourself, and how can you make it up to others, and resolve to do better, if you've been shortchanging others?

REIN IT IN: If it's necessary to rein your ego in, try reading a book like *Mistakes Were Made (but Not by Me)* by Carol Tavris, PhD, and Elliot Aronson, PhD; *Blind Spots: Why Smart People Do Dumb Things,* by Madeleine L. Van Hecke, PhD; or *The How of Happiness: A New Approach to Getting the Life You Want* by Sonja Lyubomirsky, PhD, to learn techniques for listening instead of talking and for taking in more perspectives than your own.

When you learn to notice your POWER becoming unstable, in ego or in any of the other traits we'll discuss, you can correct your course and begin to avoid falling victim to your own personality traits. Remember, all these traits can work for you as well as against you! A healthy ego leads to accomplishment, joy, healthy relationships, and work-life balance. If you do the work of regaining equilibrium and POWER, you can avoid the arrogance that is a hallmark of fragile high self-esteem and become your authentic, healthy-ego-possessing self. As Polonius says in *Hamlet*, "To thine own self be true, and it doth follow, as the night the day, thou canst not then be false to any man." That's the one un-jokey moment in a comic speech. Even a doddering goofball character can tell us how vital the need for self-assessment and true self-evaluation are, unalloyed by layers of blind ego.

2.

DENIAL

EYES WIDE SHUT

The Executive Vice President insisted he was simply a target. His status and being recently divorced singled him out. Still, after further discussion he admitted that he was friendly with the female employees but suggested it made the workplace more fun for them. He found it hard to believe that any of the women could have a problem with his behavior because they all seemed to enjoy his occasional attention. He was sure that it had to be a simple misunderstanding by the woman who was threatening a sexual harassment suit. When I told him that two other women, who had moved to another department, were also thinking about joining in the possible lawsuit he honestly seemed stunned.

There's a good chance we have all, at some time or another, been in a state of denial, usually out of fear of facing the truth, and often we don't realize it until after the fact. Sometimes we fall into a state of denial not out of fear, but out of magical thinking—a mistaken belief that we will somehow be exempt from the consequences that others face. Think of the young person who texts and drives—in the moment, the need to communicate about a party or something about what ever boy, overtakes what she knows on some level: that texting and driving kills people just like her. Sometimes, as with people who refuse to quit smoking regardless of the proven dangers, drifting into denial is a defense mechanism. Because they doubt their ability to quit, they alter their belief ("I won't get lung cancer") to suit what they know they're going to do anyway (continue smoking).

Denial can be a good thing if it allows you to take an exciting risk in the face of the likelihood that it won't pay off, or if it allows you to hope against hope that the person you love will be one of the rare few who beat Stage 4 cancer. Your denial can help you get through that tough time, and even confer healing optimism to your loved one, precisely because your belief in a long-shot outcome is sincere. It can work as a great motivator and offer us the freedom to explore, because denial gives us a delightfully unrealistic perspective on our chances of success. Would some of the most successful companies in the world have ever been founded if entrepreneurs weren't able to push aside the odds of failure? In such circumstances denial is a short-term coping strategy that allows us to reach for our goal as opposed to a long-term strategy that almost inevitably leads to destructive behavior and negative consequences, as well as prevents constructive action to address the problem.

Denial in its most beneficial form is a can-do attitude, a

positive refusal to dwell on obstacles, and a motivational energy to chip away at those obstacles, all while not internalizing the likelihood that they could get the best of you. It's when denial goes too far, however, that it can lead to disaster for everyone. I've seen many examples in my work of people who fail to acknowledge a deep truth or misread signs that should put them on high alert, refusing to see what is evident to most others, or anything contrary to their own beliefs. This is denial mixed with ego, and it is a potent combination: It protects a false image of yourself and allows the irresponsible behavior to take place and continue for years, especially if those around you enable you to maintain your denial.

This chapter focuses on how denial can sometimes be necessary to help you cope with life. It will also show, however, that most of the time, denial fuels crisis through distortion, justification, and excusing away the problem. I'll address the ways that denial is expressed and then highlight examples from some notorious case studies. Throughout this chapter, I hope to give you a better understanding of how internal and external factors affect the way our minds receive and process information and can therefore prevent us from being honest with ourselves and others. Finally, I'll close with the POWER model to give you a real-life example of how we can work to overcome negative denial in our lives.

When Denial Is a Good Motivator
Let's start with a deeper look at what is good about denial, and how you can cultivate a healthy sense of denial—the kind

of denial that will get you through tough times and enable you to take risks.

Almost any personal ambition requires some form of denial when the goal is to succeed in something that relatively few people are able to do. You'll never take a risk in a risky world if you don't employ a little denial to buffer the thought that you'll most likely fail. If Steve Jobs and Steve Wozniak hadn't had the gumption to start Apple in a garage with almost no resources, their company would never have grown into the powerhouse it is today, and millions of lives would not have been changed for the better. Actors, musicians, athletes, and fine artists all know, on some level, that the odds of making a living in their chosen field are extremely low. They have to believe that they can buck the odds in order to make the attempt—and without the attempt, of course, they most certainly will not succeed.

The key to a healthy denial is to wear blinders—not to be blind. You have to be aware of the odds, even as you deny and then defy them, and then do everything you can to make success a probability. I find denial most useful when it concerns not accepting your own limitations. Being in denial about the possibility for success of a far-fetched plan can help us to challenge the status quo, and it can also often lead to expanding our understanding of a subject or some given knowledge. How many scientific discoveries and breakthroughs owe their existence to someone simply saying, "No, I don't believe that"?

On a personal level, by denying the labels society applies to us, we are motivated to extend beyond their boundaries.

A person with a disability may not benefit by focusing on the limiting nature of his or her condition. Accepting the statistics or prognosis about the trajectory of a disease may be more harmful than helpful if it causes the person to simply give up on life. Sometimes denial lets us put off what we may be incapable of accepting until we can. But if denial enables people to file the information that doesn't help them in a part of their brains where it can remain contained, and then to focus their energy on the things they can control, sometimes the positive action they take allows them to overcome the odds that are stacked against them.

Erik Weihenmayer is a good example of exactly this. Erik had a disease of the retina that he knew meant he'd eventually lose his sight, which he did at the age of thirteen. Erik refused to learn braille or how to walk with a cane, and no doubt some in his family correctly saw this as a denial of his reality. But Erik was also able to channel this denial of the limitations of his condition to achieve something that the majority of sighted people would never even attempt: to climb Mount Everest. This is a grueling feat for even experienced climbers who have every one of their senses at their disposal; to achieve it without any visual perception was considered almost impossible. All the odds were seemingly against him. Erik knew all the reasons why this might not be a good idea—however, he also believed that he could accomplish this monumental task. On May 25, 2001, after a grueling journey, Erik became the first and only blind person to reach the summit of Mount Everest.

Denial allowed Erik to focus his energy on what he could

control—learning how to climb, preparing for his climb up Everest—while not wasting his reserves on that which he couldn't (he couldn't change the fact of his blindness). But what is clear is that Erik didn't pretend he wasn't going blind; instead, he refused to accept the limitations of blindness that most people associate with the condition.

The ABCs of Denial

As helpful as a degree of denial can be in getting through life, I usually am called in to help clients once their state of denial has gotten them into trouble—after they have been unable to read the writing on the wall and accept the severity of a situation. It is part of my job to repair their reputations after the denial has done its damage. But living in a state of denial is essentially spinning ourselves. When we lie to ourselves or sell ourselves a limited view of a situation out of fear or an inability to change, in the long term this behavior can become a prescription for crisis.

There are three different ways denial typically shows itself: in our affect, in our behavior, and in our cognition, or the way we think.

Let's start with affective indicators of denial: This is when our responses are emotionally inappropriate to the potential seriousness of a situation. Laughing when something obviously isn't funny is one common way that people express their level of denial. For instance, consider the small-business owner who, when addressing employees' fears about the company's solvency, laughs off a probable bankruptcy and jokes about how everything is fine instead of discussing their concerns. Or when someone is in a weirdly, relentlessly upbeat mood when his wife is packing to move out, this is a sign that he's not accepting the situation and his emotions have yet to align themselves with reality. Affective displays of denial are relatively uncommon.

Behavioral indicators of denial are more typical. An alcoholic who continues to party with his friends in bars and nightclubs every weekend, even when it's clear that there's a problem, is exhibiting denial through his behavior. Behavioral denial can be particularly destructive, at least preventing you from doing what you need to be doing to improve your circumstances, and at worst causing lasting harm.

Last, cognitive indicators of denial "are a form of defense that rely on selective attention and the narrowing of one's perceptual field," as one study put it. In other words, cognitive denial is when we see only what we want to see. For instance, an aging athlete whose skill has deteriorated but who focuses on the occasional good performance as proof that there is still gas in the tank is in cognitive denial.

These three indicators of denial often work together to fuel the mistaken beliefs and contribute to unbalanced denial. Let's now turn to the ways in which I've seen people slip into states of denial that have led to disasters, ones that could have been avoided.

Common Denial Belief 1: I can't believe it is happening, so it's simply not happening.

Consider, for example, the friend of a colleague of mine who called me because she had just gotten fired from a huge company. She was mortified, completely stunned that this had happened to her, and asked me, essentially, to make it look as if she hadn't been fired. When we talked about what had happened, she spoke about how she had never seen the ax swinging for her neck. I asked her a series of questions to get to the bottom of what had taken place. She told me that she'd been getting excluded from meetings—they'd change the time and "forget" to tell her or say she didn't need to be present. She shrugged it off, even laughed about it. This is a classic case of affective denial. She was being essentially demoted right before her eyes, but denied it to herself. Instead of reporting to the president, suddenly she was reporting to someone a level down—there was another layer of management in her way. And oh, they'd cut the budget for her project. She took all this as it came—showing signs of behavioral denial—spinning it to herself as simply the vagaries of working in a corporate structure. She simply did not take in that this was writing on the wall—in big, block capital letters.

To me, it was obvious that the company had been slowly but steadily phasing her out; from where I stood, it took an impressive level of denial for her not to see it. Had she been able to see it, she could have immediately gone to her boss and said, "I used to report directly to you; is there a reason I'm now reporting to X?" Either her boss could have told her why this change was made and she could have seized the opportunity to show him that she could fix whatever problem he perceived or, at the very least, she would not have been blindsided and could have set herself up better to find other employment. If she had an inkling she was being excluded from planning sessions intentionally, even if she wasn't sure, she might have said, "I want to make sure you have access to my calendar, so whenever you want to schedule a meeting you can make sure I'm available." If she wasn't being excluded on purpose, no harm done, but if she was, she could let those around her know she was alert, part of the team, and not one to be cut out of important discussions. I also thought that she should have spent more time cultivating work relationships and not isolating herself. Often, others can help us see things that we cannot see for ourselves. It was too late for me to advise her on how to head the problem off at the pass, but I hope you'll benefit from what I wish I could have told her.

Common Denial Belief 2: I am the exception.

Denial begins with what I consider the ultimate spin, believing that whatever negative behavior you're engaged in won't catch up with you. It can be because you think you're too smart, or your status is too great, or your wealth will let you buy your way out of it, or any number of similar factors. This is cognitive denial, and it usually results from denial plus ego. That's why it's important to have people around you who offer honest opinions, even if they tell you something you don't want to hear.

People, sometimes celebrities in particular, live in environments that conspire to keep the denial going on every front. I unfortunately have seen a lot of people who surround themselves with others who enable them to continue their destructive behavior. This also happens all the time where there is a collective denial of the fact that one group member has a problem with substance abuse. For example, Michael Jackson appeared to be surrounded by people who supported his state of denial on many levels. After his death and the trial of his personal physician, Conrad Murray, it became clear that those around him were ineffective in piercing his bubble of denial, or they didn't try to make him see that he was in trouble. Murray most certainly was engaging in harmful—indeed deadly—accommodation, a topic we address in an upcoming chapter. Jackson was not, in fact, the exception to the rule that drug abuse is dangerous, as he must have believed on some level.

Common Denial Belief 3: Everybody else says things are fine, so they are.

When people around us are in cahoots with our personal denial, it becomes much easier for an individual to adhere to mistaken beliefs. The case of celebrities being surrounded by disciples is a form of this, although sometimes, the hangers-on are not in true denial themselves—they are simply cynically (and perhaps unconsciously) supporting the denial of the celebrity for their own gain. If a star quits the business, sobers up, and starts living the quiet life, a decision which would be healthiest for that person, the gravy train would stop running.

To prevent that from happening, the entourage may support that person's denial and tell her everything is fine, she doesn't have a problem. That's exactly what the celebrity wants to hear, and so she believes it.

What's harder still is when a group of people truly believes something that is not the case—a group state of denial, as it were. They shut their eyes to what is plainly happening, and individual denial by each member of the group becomes a culture of denial. The consequences of denial are amplified if decisions are made by an entire group of people—an organization or an institution—all using this defense mechanism at the same time. A free-thinking person might feel pressured to conform to the group denial, and someone who is in denial herself might find it harder than usual to break out of it without the perspective of others.

In 1972, Yale University researcher Irving Janis coined the term "groupthink": "a mode of thinking that people engage in when they are deeply involved in a cohesive in-group, when the members' strivings for unanimity override their motivation to realistically appraise alternative courses of action." According to Janis, groupthink occurs when "concurrence-seeking tendencies lead a group member to openly agree with the perceived group position even if a group member privately disagrees." Groupthink produces defective decision-making, especially when the group is in collective denial. Groupthink occurs when members in a cohesive group unconsciously try to create an illusion of unanimity toward what is perceived to be the group's position—sometimes at the expense of what the individual believes to be right. Pressure situations are notorious for producing groupthink. Those within the group or organization have "unquestioned belief" and an "illusion of invulnerability." The "illusion of unanimity," in which it seems as though others are all agreeing, discourages dissenters, who are seen as disruptive and disloyal—even if they are the only ones seeing reality.

One of the most glaring examples of groupthink's denial leading to a crisis is the Catholic Church. In the late 1990s and early 2000s, reports publicly began to surface concerning inappropriate contact between mostly young male parishioners and Catholic priests. What was slowly becoming apparent was that these were not isolated incidents. Instead, what the nation and world were witnessing was an institutional scandal that had been systematically ignored, concealed, and denied by the Catholic Church. Individuals had come forward with claims of abuse, but the group denial of the institution ensured that they were silenced or made to question their own realities.

The abuse was not confined to the United States alone. In 2009, a scathing seven-hundred-page report on the Catholic archdiocese of Dublin was commissioned by the Irish government and concluded that the Church was most concerned with "the maintenance of secrecy, the avoidance of scandal, the protection of the reputation of the church, and the preservation of its assets." These are some of the same reasons individuals cling to denial—they don't want to lose what they stand for if they face reality.

The report was full of incidents that not only should have raised concern but should have warranted immediate and decisive actions. The report included specific examples such as that of Father James McNamee, who had over twenty-one complaints lodged against him between 1950 and 1979. What is really astonishing is the complacency and outright failure to act of those in positions of authority. Numerous officials, operating at different levels of the Church hierarchy, turned a blind eye, refused to acknowledge suspicious behavior, and attempted to protect themselves and the Church before protecting McNamee's victims. In fact, as reported by the *New York Times*, "only 20 percent of the 3,000 accused priests whose cases went to the church's doctrinal office between 2001 and 2010 were given full church trials, and only some of those were defrocked."

Over the course of two decades the Church, as a collective, continued to be in denial about a serious problem they had, and this required hundreds of individual acts of denial. Church officials received thousands of complaints about clergy accused of inappropriate sexual behavior with children but did nothing to acknowledge the severity of the accusations. In one such case, a cardinal ignored letters and complaints and ultimately failed to defrock a Wisconsin priest who was alleged to have molested up to two hundred deaf boys. Instead of being disciplined or tried, the priest was transferred out of his parish but still was able to work, unsupervised, with children. The series of decisions that were made by multiple people involved denial on a monumental scale—denying that these allegations might have merit, that the priest might repeat the behavior, and that the Church would be called to account for its decisions. It is truly staggering. The larger denial this case represents is a denial of the fact that the rules within and for the Church are subject to the rules of the society at large. That was one of the most galling denials of all.

No doubt, the Church was concerned with the effect that a scandal would have on its image. It was already facing declining membership and was struggling to hold on to legitimacy in a world that was becoming increasingly secular. Sadly, the terrible response to the abuse crisis, on top of the abuse stories themselves, probably became an additional reason why some members walked away from the Church. The Church has only recently taken steps to address the concerns of victims, a sign that the culture of denial might be slowly changing.

The problem with the Catholic Church was that in its denial it sought to protect itself instead of doing what should have been the priority and duty—protecting the victims. In the time officials spent denying reality because it didn't conform to what they cared to believe about the Church, thousands of children were traumatized and the reputation of the Church—and many honest, decent members of the clergy—was forever destroyed.

I can't speak to what should have happened in the Church to keep so many children from having so many devastating experiences; that's an incredibly complex question that I'm not in a position to try to answer. There's no doubt that when repeated abuse allegations were made, simply denying any wrongdoing was not the answer. I believe that the phenomenon of groupthink prolonged the total lack of leadership that led to the continued abuses and the public relations crisis that the Church found itself in as word of its cover-up got out. As a result, the Church lost some of the moral authority that it so desperately was trying to protect.

You may think that you are immune to groupthink—that as a strong-minded individual, you would never allow yourself to be so "weak" or manipulated by others. However, consider the following experiment, first performed by Solomon Asch, a pioneer in social psychology. In Asch's experiments, performed at Swarthmore College in the 1950s, eight participants were gathered in a room and asked to look at a group of lines projected on a screen. A researcher then went around the room and asked participants, one by one, to match a line projected on the screen to one of three comparison lines also projected on the screen. He then repeated this process several times. The length of the lines was distinctly different and there was clearly only one right answer to the question. The twist to this experiment, however, was that of the eight participants in the study, only one of them was an actual subject, and he was the last person asked to match the lines. The other seven were planted there to purposely give the wrong answer. Asch was testing whether, given these circumstances, the participant would bow to the pressure and conform to the false perceptions of the group. Thirty-three percent conformed to the erroneous majority more than half of the time and 75 percent of the participants changed their answers at least once to conform to the group's consensus—even though it was clearly wrong.

Common Denial Belief 4: Things aren't changing, so I don't need to adapt.

Groups and individuals are resistant to change, and that may simply be human nature. But just because it's understandable and happens a lot doesn't mean that it can't lead to dangerous denial. Take a look at the record industry, which was in denial about the changing landscape upon which it needed to conduct business, and so clung to old ideas that no longer worked. Such collective denial had negative ramifications for the entire business of music.

Once upon a time, back in the days before the Internet—indeed, when record companies actually put out records on vinyl—record companies nurtured bands, signed a variety of new acts, and helped them grow. Now record companies focus their spending only on their biggest acts. Longtime paradigms of music distribution have been dismantled. The business has been fractured and decentralized. Bands put out their own music online; people make their own playlists instead of listening to the radio; kids download music legally (and illegally) and swap hard drives loaded with music. It was clear to many analysts looking objectively at the industry that things were changing and that the industry needed to adapt to the new reality, rather than deny it and cling to the old methods of doing things.

They didn't. For years record executives seemed more focused on punishing the people who took advantage of the new technology than on developing new business models. The industry has had a hard time creating new business models that worked; as a result many companies have simply folded.

A digital privacy expert I know likes to say, "You have to make it easier to buy than it is to steal." Obviously, that task requires a lot of creative, innovative thinking, which involves an admission—not a denial—that the problem was the fact that the industry wasn't yet on top of how to sell in this new environment. It didn't rest with the "thieves" (who were less interested in the legality of what they were doing than in trying to get music for as little money as possible). This can't have been a popular opinion, either, at the dawn of the digital music age; imagine how hard it must have been in the room at a multimillion-dollar company trying to convince the CEO that it was all going to come crashing down. So many companies did the less confrontational thing and assured themselves that the right thing to do was to fight the people pirating the music rather than fight for a way to make it easier to buy. iTunes, under the supervision of visionary Steve Jobs, figured out a way to successfully integrate the new technology, acknowledging the changing landscape, and developed a convenient way for people to get authorized access to the music and pay for it.

Most of us experiencing conformity through denial mechanisms will not be responsible for major catastrophes. However, when we are at work pushing through a project, making decisions about the direction of a company, or voting on a policy at a PTA meeting, we all need to be aware that we could be mindlessly following the will of the majority and therefore not processing information correctly; at this point we need to step back and assess the situation before making potentially poor decisions. Most important, we need to look at the situation as it changes, rather than cling to an idea that no longer works, simply because we lack the vision to make a change.

Common Denial Belief 5: If I don't look too closely, it'll all work out.

Sometimes, when we desperately want to believe something is true, we simply shut our eyes to information that's right in front of us. At other times, we negligently fail to seek it out, or do our due diligence. This, to me, is a form of denial, and it can certainly lead to crisis, both personal and professional. It involves ignoring your own instincts, and sometimes ignoring the voices of more cautious, clearer-thinking people around you.

I was once at a bridal shower with about twenty-five other women. I was trying to be social, even though it was at a spa and I was distracted by the very real possibility that someone would try to make me have a mud wrap. At one point, a woman I'd never met announced that she'd just gotten engaged. Everyone began exclaiming, "Ooh! Yay! Show us the ring!" It turned out she was an actress and he was a "financial management" guy and they'd gotten engaged four weeks after they'd met. As everyone else congratulated the new bride-to-be, my immediate reaction—it burst out of my mouth the second it hit my brain—was: "Are you out of your mind? Did you do a background check?" Everyone fell silent.

I didn't know many of the women there, which might have made it easier for me to voice my opinion. I may not have been the most popular woman there at that moment, but I stood by what I said. Although it clearly made the woman uneasy, my friend made the effort to deflect the tension by claiming I was the cynical and paranoid type. But really, I'm not. I didn't know for sure, but I suspected that the bride-to-be was so attached to the belief that she finally had what she wanted that she, in my opinion, leapt before she looked, which is one behavioral form of denial. She wanted the fairy tale—she was fifty years old in a business that prizes youth, and she'd been in a series of bad relationships with self-absorbed actors. In her worldview, this financially solvent guy had to be Prince Charming. And maybe he really was. But my attitude was, well, why not be sure? If she rushed into this marriage without actually acknowledging that things were moving fast—and if she got defensive about the idea that there might be things she'd want to know about the man she was planning to spend the rest of her life with—there had to be a level of denial operating.

I don't know if she ever did run a background check but the last I heard she and her fiancé had decided to wait a year or two before actually having the wedding. That, to me, indicates that they had decided to not get caught up in the fantasy of the moment. I sincerely wish them the best of luck.

Why do people not look too closely? I believe it's usually because they want to believe that even if something looks too good to be true, that it miraculously is. And it might be—some marriages that take place after a four-week engagement do, in fact, work out. But as I would suggest to all my clients, we all need to heed this advice: If something seems too good to be true then it probably is. Denial causes us to believe what we want to believe—and more than that, it can cause us to convince ourselves that what we're looking at is not belief at all, but a fact.

A vivid and infamous example of this is Bernie Madoff and his $65 billion Ponzi scheme. Madoff built his business, legally at first, by trading stocks cheaply. In 1997, through a series of federal regulatory changes, the rules governing the way trading worked shifted, and Madoff's profit margins diminished. He couldn't legally make money the way he had before. If he wanted to earn for his investors at the same rate, he had to do something else. Perhaps that was when he lost his moral compass. Or perhaps he'd been laying the groundwork for a hustle since the 1970s. In any case, he built a pyramid-scheme business, which before long was propping up his legal trading business.

It's easy to see what made Madoff's firm so attractive. Most of his clients came to him through private referrals and word-of-mouth. This unofficial social membership came with the understanding that no one looked too closely at exactly how he was investing. Because the returns were so high, this was not a problem that needed much enforcing. No one wanted to become a social pariah and be left out of the financial fairyland that Madoff promised and was apparently delivering. Not only did this keep Madoff's scheming under the radar, but it probably contributed to the investors' denial of the facts.

In May of 2001, several reports surfaced that questioned the legitimacy of Madoff's business, but even after SEC investigations in 2001, investors were still very happy to leave their money with Madoff. Ignoring the signs, ignoring all the evidence before them, the investors turned a blind eye and refused to see the landscape. It was definitely too good to be true.

Madoff's investors believed because they wanted to believe. They wanted those incredibly high returns. Yes, a lot of his investors didn't understand finance and would just shrug and say their money was in the hands of a master. But the reason Madoff was in demand was that he was getting his clients impossible returns—10, 15, even 20 percent a year, every year, no matter what was happening in the market.

How was it that everyone believed this guy could keep on getting statistically impossible financial returns—returns unlike anything anyone else was getting, and with clockwork-like regularity—for decades? His accounting firm employed just one accountant!

As the author of the book *Wizard of Lies,* Diana Henriques, explains, despite his outright lies and outrageous claims, Madoff's investors were willing to believe the lie. They were the elite of the world, not the people who are normally thought to be victims of such schemes. They believed that they were invulnerable, and it was that false sense of security that might have contributed to the denial that left them all so exposed. Obviously, even the smart, rich, and famous are not immune to denial.

Ultimately Madoff's juggling act fell apart, as it inevitably had to. When some investors finally decided to take out their money as the economy was heading south in 2008, Madoff couldn't handle the requests for redemptions. There was nothing there; the profits were smoke and mirrors. Madoff supposedly wrote $173 million in checks to his family and close friends, then confessed. He was arrested and pleaded guilty to eleven felonies and was sentenced to a hundred and fifty years in prison, the maximum penalty.

If only Madoff's victims had assessed the environment and examined their own denial of the laws of probability! If only they'd heeded the words of financial fraud advisers like Harry Markopolos, who'd been asserting for years that Madoff's model was statistically impossible. At the time, Markopolos was an independent fraud investigator who over a nine-year period was relentless in urging the Securities and Exchange Commission to investigate Madoff. There were also other journalists and reports that called into question Madoff's integrity. Yet Madoff's victims selectively deferred to certain experts and certain sources rather than take in the whole picture. Perhaps these investors refused to believe that someone as accomplished as Madoff could be incompetent. So they went along and trusted his judgment. As long as the money kept rolling in, they turned off their critical faculties. The challenge for all of us is to keep asking questions when something doesn't pass the smell test.

Denial is everywhere in the Madoff case, evidenced in the minds of the victims; Madoff's family, who claim not to have had knowledge of his schemes (though one wonders whether they simply believed what they wanted to believe); and Madoff himself, who had to have been laboring under a massive veil of denial to think that he would be able to get away with his huge, destructive fraud. Madoff, exhibiting affective and cognitive denial, blames the success of his Ponzi scheme on those individuals and institutions that turned a blind eye to his business practices. In fact, Madoff told the *New York Times* that the banks and hedge funds he invested for showed "willful blindness." They failed to do their own due diligence; they should have known. "They had to know," Madoff told the *Times*. "But the attitude was sort of, 'If you're doing something wrong, we don't want to know.'" That's denial in action. Madoff exhibits what researchers David Matza and Gresham Sykes refer to as techniques of neutralization. He denied responsibility, which prevented him from feeling guilt. He denied injury to his victims by neutralizing or minimizing the extent of their losses.

I tell my clients that they must use their own critical faculties and do their own research when someone offers them something that sounds too good to be true. In this world, there are very few sure things, so I urge them to constantly evaluate the landscape: If something seems off, explore it. Even if that process is difficult and isn't pointing to the outcome you want. If you invested time in something or someone, don't continue on a potentially harmful course because you are too embarrassed to admit you may have made a mistake. And if you are someone who knows the truth about a misleading situation, do something about it now. The longer you keep it up or allow the scheme to be kept up, the harder it will be to get out.

Common Denial Belief 6: I want it badly enough that anything I do to get it is OK.

There were many motivations that fueled Madoff's denial, and the pressure of the expectations brought on by success was no doubt among them. There may have been a part of him that simply couldn't bear to own up to the idea that he wasn't the genius everyone thought he was. This was certainly the case with a young woman with talent, intelligence, and the resources to succeed, Kaavya Viswanathan. I believe that her desire to succeed, probably wrought of pressure from her parents and her own expectations, led her to deny that she couldn't achieve what she set out to do, and then to further use denial to explain away the lies she perpetrated to cover it up. It was heartbreaking to witness in someone so young.

Viswanathan was an author who received a book deal just after graduating from high school. The daughter of a neurosurgeon and a doctor-turned-stay-at-home-mom, she was determined to attend an Ivy League school. The editor in chief of her high school newspaper, she showed her writing to the top-tier college admissions consultant her parents hired, who hooked Viswanathan up with an agent, and the girl received a six-figure, two-book deal. *How Opal Mehta Got Kissed, Got Wild, and Got a Life* was published in 2006, during Viswanathan's freshman year at Harvard. It's the story of an Indian-American girl who is a plugger and a chugger (in the parlance of college admissions officers), a grind. When a Harvard admissions officer tells her she's not well-rounded, she becomes determined to lighten up and discover shopping, frivolity, fun. Viswanathan said the book came from her own experience, and parts of it may have been. But it turned out over forty passages were plagiarized from the works of a popular young adult author, Megan McCafferty.

At first, Viswanathan blamed her "photographic memory," saying she must have somehow internalized McCafferty's books, which she'd loved in high school. Then it was discovered that the book also contained phrases and passages from the works of writers Sophie Kinsella, Meg Cabot, Salman Rushdie, and Tanuja Desai Hidier. The publisher withdrew the book and canceled Viswanathan's contract. The shame and embarrassment Viswanathan suffered had to have been unbearable, especially for someone surrounded by such high expectations.

What was she thinking? We could argue that she didn't know better. We might also blame ego or ambition for the troubles of plagiarists like Viswanathan. Did her fragile high self-esteem, discussed in the last chapter, make her need acclaim so desperately that she'd steal out of fear that her own writing wasn't good enough? Had she been pushed so hard toward excellence that she felt that cheating was the only way out?

Even if you give credence to all of the above, there's no question that denial was her downfall. My suspicion is that Viswanathan panicked under the weight of the expectations she put on herself and she made a terrible decision to steal the work of others. Then she made a conscious choice not to think about what she was doing, and immersed herself in denial about her behavior. I suspect that at some point she knew her actions were wrong, but she was so used to being successful that she felt entitled to success, however she attained it. When she found herself in over her head, she did not consider all of the options—asking for an extension on her due date, asking for help writing the book, talking to others about ways to get through the writing process. Instead, she focused on the fact that she needed to finish the book and wanted it to be really good. She may have been insecure about her own abilities, despite all her accomplishments, enough so that she deluded herself into thinking that the thoughts of others were her own.

I wonder if a lack of a sense of self, the pressure and expectation to succeed, and the threat to her identity made it impossible for her to even admit the truth to herself. The truth is that sometimes our denials are so profound that we truly delude ourselves into believing that we are telling the truth—even when all the facts point to the contrary. In addition to the pressure to achieve, I also think some of Viswanathan's denial comes from the inability to reconcile the fact that she was a supposedly bright young lady attending one of the most prestigious institutions in the world but at the same time could not meet the pressures of finishing an original work. Instead of copping to the facts, which would label her a failure, which didn't fit into her self-image, she simply blamed her photographic memory—which is much more consistent with the image she may have had of herself. She needed an excuse that did not upset her positive and attractive self-image.

Viswanathan undoubtedly was dealing with conflicting thoughts as she "wrote" and researched her novel. Paying attention to these conflicting thoughts, rather than quashing them and forging ahead, could have helped her overcome her inability to accept responsibility before it was too late.

Common Denial Belief 7: Cognitive dissonance.

In *Mistakes Were Made,* Tavris and Aronson define cognitive dissonance as "a state of tension that occurs whenever a person holds two cognitions (ideas, attitudes, beliefs, opinions) that are psychologically inconsistent, such as 'Smoking is a dumb thing to do because it could kill me' and 'I smoke two packs a day.'" The dissonance in our brains makes us uncomfortable. "Dissonance is disquieting because to hold two ideas that contradict each other is to flirt with absurdity," Tavris and Aronson write. "And, as Albert Camus observed, we humans are creatures who spend our lives trying to convince ourselves that our existence is not absurd."

Ted Haggard and his wife, Gayle, are excellent examples of what I'm talking about. Ted Haggard was an evangelical minister in New Life Church in Colorado Springs, Colorado. At one time he led a megachurch congregation of over ten thousand worshippers. However, in 2006, Ted stepped down (or, rather, was ousted) from his pastoral duties thanks to a controversy ignited by Mike Jones. Jones was a male escort who claimed Haggard had engaged his services for the past three years. Haggard was known to Jones as "Art." In a very

Clintonesque statement, Haggard claims that he never had "sex sex" but he did confess to "sexual immorality."

The most obvious aspect of Haggard's cognitive dissonance is that, despite having engaged in a homosexual liaison, he maintained he was strictly heterosexual. His mind couldn't reconcile the fact of his having engaged in homosexual activities with his belief system that said homosexuality is a sin, so he simply denied that his actions meant that he was gay.

After his confession, Ted entered counseling to address what he referred to as "sexual temptations" and upon completion of the program, his representatives told the *Denver Post* that he was "completely heterosexual." There was obviously a lot more to the story than Haggard was letting on. For instance, he later admitted in a *GQ* interview that if he were younger, without a family and kids, he would "probably" identify himself as a bisexual. Furthermore, after the Jones confessions, additional allegations circulated around New Life Church and the community from a young male volunteer who claimed that Haggard had taken advantage of him in a counseling session.

Ted's wife, Gayle, was also wrapped up in denial. Through all the turmoil and embarrassment of these allegations Gayle stayed by his side. The questions about Ted Haggard's sexuality were not new to Gayle—they now were just public. As Gayle stated in an interview on the *Today* show, her husband had a homosexual affair early on in their marriage: "I think at that point I was ignorant of the gravity. . . . I felt as though, you know, we all struggle, you know, in different areas of our lives and certainly in our sexuality, so I was willing to forgive him. . . . I felt as though the problem was pretty much solved. . . . But it would reemerge in his life from time to time and he wouldn't tell me about it." In other words, her husband's homosexual tendencies didn't jibe with her belief system, so she saw them as a lapse, not part of who he was.

In interviews with various media figures, Gayle appeared oddly calm and forgiving about the whole incident. In her book *Why I Stayed,* Gayle said that she firmly believed in her marriage. If she left her husband, then she would be "illustrating that some people mess up too badly to be redeemed . . . And I don't believe that. I don't believe in throwing people away because they've sinned, because all people are valuable and loved by God." Throughout an interview with Fox News's Mike Huckabee, Gayle spoke with a soft voice and a smile plastered on her face the entire time—even when talking about what her husband had been accused of.

Some may look at Gayle as heroic, a true example of what a Christian should be: someone willing to forgive her husband for the ultimate betrayal. And that may be so, but her forgiveness, which seems to require that she accept that her husband is not, in fact, bisexual, strikes me as an act of profound denial as well.

The Haggard marriage, I believe, is an extreme example of two people reinforcing one another's denial. Ted's denial cost him his church and the trust of many around him. Gayle claims to be happy, but watching her interviews, I sometimes wonder how much she must endure every day as people around her doubt fundamental aspects of her marriage. Cognitive dissonance made them both rationalize questionable behavior and helped them justify their commitment to each other, but living this way is a very difficult thing to sustain.

Common Denial Behavior 8: Everything's under control, I'm not addicted.

Admitting to being addicted to something—indeed, owning up to engaging in any behavior we cannot control—is a very difficult thing to do. Doing so feels like an admission of weakness, and of course an addiction is by definition something we believe we cannot give up so the thought of having to is enough to deter us. "I don't have a problem," is what we tell ourselves and others, because owning that you have a problem likely means taking a step toward doing something about it, which raises the question: How will I live without drugs, alcohol, or sex, whatever it is I need in order to function?

Perhaps one of the saddest high-profile examples of denial of addiction is the actress and singer Lindsay Lohan. She has been acting most of her life but she became a household name after the hit movie *Mean Girls*. Unfortunately, she soon was becoming known for her antics offscreen, all the while denying that she was doing anything out of the ordinary for a young woman in Hollywood.

It didn't help that those around her made excuses for her behavior. But even when Lindsay was directly confronted with the way that her destructive habits were ruining her career when a studio executive made public a letter calling her on-set behavior "irresponsible and unprofessional," the denial that fueled her addiction was impossible to penetrate. It became harder and harder for her to get work, but she still did not answer the wake-up call.

Lindsay was accused in the media of having a gamut of illnesses that seem to be standard for young starlets these days: eating disorders, drug addiction, cutting, and other destructive behaviors. Lindsay denied them all. Even after numerous photographs showed her fluctuating weight, her drinking in clubs, her stumbling home early in the morning, Lindsay claimed she was sober, healthy, and simply living life. Anything that appeared negative or questionable could easily be explained: She claimed that when she stumbled or tripped, she was actually pushed; when reports surfaced that she had arrived late to a photo shoot that was being filmed by a reality show, she declared it was because the show's network "set her up" to look irresponsible by giving her the wrong call time. Many people noted that even after her latest stint of court-ordered counseling, Lindsay still continued to be photographed on the party scene. Her behavior has, unequivocally, prevented her from becoming the next big star that Hollywood once predicted she would be. And yet she—and the people around her—seems to be in total denial about the negative impact her lifestyle choices have had on her potential to ever be considered a serious actress.

The denial of addiction is not the exclusive domain of celebrities. We all know folks who deny eating disorders, affairs, gambling addiction, and drug abuse. They always have an answer as to why their behavior is justified, or they simply deny that it's taking place. Whatever the drug of choice, it becomes a problem when it disrupts their everyday lives and they blame everything and everyone else, assuring people that the situation makes complete sense given the unique circumstances of their lives.

People with a loved one in crisis can be victims of denial too—they enable the person or they see only what they want to see, as seems to be the case with Lindsay's mother, who has repeatedly written off her daughter's critics as too hard on her. Even if they know their loved one is in crisis, they may decide not to rock the boat and make waves. Why? Because it's uncomfortable. Confrontation causes us to change the dynamic of a relationship and may, in fact, ruin the relationship altogether. Yet if a life is to be saved then often that is the chance we must take.

Might you have a problem with addiction? Ask yourself whether there's anything you routinely hide from family, friends, or co-workers: liquor bottles, off-track betting receipts, pill bottles, cigarette butts, empty ice cream containers? Do you tell yourself that yes, you gamble a lot, but at least you win more often than you lose? Have you ever missed a family event or been late to work because of your indulgences? If so, you need to address the issue before it destroys your life.

The Power of Self-Justification

Whatever the reasons for your denial and however it manifests in your life—hasty marriages, addictive behavior, or job or financial loss—once you're deeply in it, it can be very hard to see a way out. We often have to fight hard against our own prodigious powers of denial, and the way we do this is by justifying our actions, good or bad.

Indeed, in order to feel good about the choices we make, self-justification is necessary. Yet mindless self-justification, or justifying things that we know were mistakes for the sake of sticking to our story, can draw us deeper into disaster. It blocks our ability to even see our errors, let alone correct them. It distorts reality, keeping us from getting all the information we need and assessing issues clearly. It prolongs and widens rifts between lovers, friends, and nations. It keeps us from letting go of unhealthy habits. It permits the guilty to avoid taking responsibility for their deeds, as when an employee is caught embezzling and he justifies it by saying he is egregiously underpaid. It's only through constant self-policing that we can make sure our self-justification is mindful and not a trip down denial.

The only antidote to denial's negative side is to be aware of our own blind spots. We need to understand our tendencies toward greed, racism, laziness, etc.—and stay alert to them. Flaws are part of human nature. Accepting this instead of denying it helps us avoid crises in the first place; if we feel no shame about our flaws, we can address them in an aboveboard way.

If some of my clients had acknowledged their own dark sides and biases, they might have avoided the situations that brought them to me in the first place. Investors talk about "chasing a loss." That's when you keep hanging on, hoping the stock picture will change, so you can buy or sell at the price you were determined to get. But the picture changes. A stock that was once worth fifty dollars a share might never see that high point again. If you cling to the hope that the stock will go up, refusing to sell as it sinks lower and lower, you're chasing a loss.

That's how denial can work, too; we hang on to dusty facts, bad business models, and incorrect self-perceptions because it seems too frightening to let go. But if we're mindful of our own biases, if we encourage ourselves to be tough but fair about our own failings, if we take deep breaths and open our minds to other people's views, we can change. We can let go of thought patterns that aren't working for us. Denial doesn't have to be devastating.

Applying the POWER Model

So how can we combat the powerful and subtle processes of personal denial and group pressure that lead us to deny what we know to be true? Let's look at the application of the POWER model to help combat denial.

Pinpoint the core trait: In this case, denial.
Own it: Acknowledge that it can be both good and bad.
Work it through: Process the role it has played in your life.
Explore it: Consider how it could play out in the future.
Rein it in: Establish how to re-achieve balance and control.

PINPOINT: When you are in a situation that seems to be spinning out of control, where decisions are being made that seem rash or uninformed, step back and isolate what is going on. Are you selectively focusing on certain evidence while ignoring other pieces of the story? Are you open to hearing dissenting opinions or are you dismissing them because they are reflecting points of view that would force you to reevaluate your actions?

OWN IT: On a personal level, this is about listening to your gut or to a trusted friend when you have a feeling you're slipping into denial. If you're in a group situation where you feel as if a poor decision is about to be made based on the group's denial, voice your concern. Point out that while consensus is good, conformity is not—and is often a direct route down the wrong path. Whether or not you think that you're on your way to a groupthink denial crisis, it's good to be aware of the conditions that are normally present during groupthink: leaders who are clearly biased toward a single course of action, a cohesive group that is also isolated from outside influence and a high-stress environment that has no formal procedures in place for exploring a variety of opinions.

WORK IT THROUGH: Make a concerted effort to separate yourself from the immediate situation. This might mean taking a mental step out of a situation to rethink something, or it could mean physically getting up and removing yourself from the group in order to collect your thoughts and reexamine the situation individually. This approach will most likely be greeted with some resistance. Oftentimes we feel pressure to make a decision in the moment; we tell ourselves and are often told by others that it's important, it can't wait, and it needs to be decided now. But a bad decision made in the heat of the moment can have longer-lasting negative effects than the time it takes to take a step back and come up with a solid, informed one. As you're working through a decision, don't be afraid to consult outside counsel—a friend, a co-worker, a family member, an impartial arbitrator who doesn't have a vested interest in the outcome. Present the information to this source and see what the response is. It's not necessarily that you are looking for agreement or disagreement; it's that you are looking for someone to challenge the assumptions that you and the group have made and view the information with a fresh pair of eyes.

EXPLORE IT: On a personal level, take the time to mentally walk through the possibility that you're in denial about whatever situation you're in. If you suspect your husband is cheating on you, and your denial is telling you to overlook signs, take a few minutes to dip your toe into the possibility that he is, and just notice what you see. You don't have to embrace that possibility right away, but ask yourself if there's a chance that it's true. Sit with any feelings that arise and see if things become clearer. In a group dynamic, ask yourself the questions that no one else is asking. Watch out for warning signals and phrases such as "This is a sure thing" or "We are 100 percent confident that this is the only way to proceed." Confidence is good, but hyperbole and all-or-nothing thinking are dangerous because they too easily discount alternative information. While you might not feel very popular being the person in the room calling for things to slow down, asking for an alternative proposal, and exploring other options, it's a whole lot better than being the person who allowed a terrible mistake to be made.

REIN IT IN: After you confront the issues of possible denial, it's time to make an informed decision. Perhaps in the end you will fall back to your original opinion, or agree with the group. Perhaps you won't. The difference is that you will have come to an informed decision not based on denial of facts and distortion of information to fit the will of the others.

3.

FEAR

STAND UP TO THE BOOGEYMAN

It was a gray, rainy day and she seemed dressed to blend in with the drabness of the weather. She looked particularly pale with no makeup on, not even lip gloss, and her hair was pulled back tightly into a bun. She appeared nervous and infrequently made eye contact. I wondered if the pressure of her recent troubles was responsible for her demeanor, or if she always dressed and inter-acted with others in this manner. She was the head accountant at an investment firm and was in trouble for not only trying to cover up the siphoning of funds by her boss but also lying about it to a grand jury. She didn't seem to be the type to be involved in something like this and had a sterling record of trust and respect-ability. She also did not take any of the money for herself. When I asked her why she got involved in all this, she said, "I had just been promoted and I was afraid if I didn't do what he told me to I would lose my job. After that I lied because I didn't want to go to jail." Sometimes, in misguided attempts to protect ourselves we end up shooting ourselves in the foot.

———

While I would not wish for anyone to live in constant fear, there's nothing like a dose of the stuff every so often to put things into perspective. As Jeff Wise, author of *Extreme Fear: The Science of Your Mind in Danger,* so eloquently puts it: "Fear is a force that gives life meaning." For those of us who are fortunate enough to have what we need, experiencing fear can help us to appreciate and clarify what is important to us. After the hell that was Hurricane Katrina, eight out of ten survivors said they had a deeper sense of purpose than they'd had before the storm. Out of their terror came clarity of purpose and an appreciation for life, friends, family, and destiny. The perspective it confers is the upside to fear that many see as a silver lining to an otherwise horrible situation.

Like most of the aspects of self we're discussing in this book, fear has its positives and negatives. Fear of consequences is a somewhat effective way to keep people in line— indeed, remind us, when we momentarily forget, that we live by a moral code. As Mark Twain once said, "There are several good protections against temptation, but the surest is cowardice." Fear of consequences helps to bring stability to our society, thereby serving the group. A prudent fear of external consequences—ideally built upon a strong foundation of fear of the guilt and discomfort of having violated our own consciences—is in part what keeps us from acting selfishly most of the time. If there were more of this kind of fear there might be less need for my services.

But despite this, for the most part, fear garners little respect. Fear is not something we feel proud of; too often we are ashamed of it. Being called a coward, a chicken, a scaredy-cat, is not exactly a badge of honor. How often do any of us admit our fears to our kids? And why don't we? This is partly because we want to spare them our fear, but also because we're ashamed. Do we ever say, "I really admire that person because she is so afraid"? But fear is an inborn instinct that goes back to the beginning of man. It is a reaction to a perceived threat that acts as our own built-in alarm system. Our brains are hardwired for it. And, as you may have surmised by now, a certain amount of fear is healthy, and keeps us from doing things that would hurt us and others. A judicious amount of fear, as well as knowing which types of fear to heed and which are merely inhibitive, can foster success in all areas of life.

In this chapter we will look at examples of fear managed positively and managed poorly, in high-profile cases involving individuals and within the infrastructure of our society and culture. We will use our POWER model to analyze some of the examples to see if what occurred improved the situation or made it worse. Then we will conclude with how to apply the model in general when dealing with fear. But first let's take a brief look at the science of fear.

What Happens When We Feel Fear

There are physiological processes that take place when we are faced with something that scares us. When we're frightened, the brain releases two groups of chemicals, endocannabinoids and opioids. As they surge through our systems, these chemicals keep us from feeling pain and give us a rush of energy and clarity that can help us when we need it most. You've heard of average-size mothers finding the strength to pull heavy objects off their children before they're crushed. That's adrenaline, one of the hormones triggered by fear. Many survivors of natural disasters and plane crashes talk about how in the heat of the moment, they just did what they had to do, without awareness of their injuries or any feeling of loss of control. In these cases, fear actually enables people to take extreme measures in order to survive.

Evolutionary theorists believe that fear is an adaptive mechanism that allows us to sense danger and respond appropriately. Indeed, if ancient peoples had walked up to the saber-toothed tiger to pet the nice kitty instead of heeding their fear and fleeing, we would not be here now. People who were appropriately scared lived to reproduce and became our ancestors, and that fear response is with us still. In studies, researchers have found that children and adults alike are quicker at identifying snakes and spiders in photos than they are at identifying benign items such as flowers. This supports the idea that humans have developed the ability to home in on targets that carry a perceived threat, especially when that target is associated with the physiological signs and feelings of fear. Fear was key to our ancestors' survival and although those same dangers are not ones we face in daily life, the mechanism of fear still works the same as it always has.

What's different now is that most of the fear we face is not physical, such as a fear of dying of exposure or of wild animals, as it was for our ancestors. Our fears are often of a psychological nature. But even when we know intellectually we are safe, our bodies will react. Back in 1872, Charles Darwin wrote about trying not to feel fear. Visiting London's Zoological Gardens, he repeatedly put his face close to the glass of an adder cage. He told himself not to flinch if the snake tried to strike. After all, the snake was behind glass! His fear was purely psychological. But he failed again and again. "As soon as the blow was struck my resolution went to nothing and I jumped a yard or two backwards with astonishing rapidity," he wrote in *The Expression of the Emotions in Man and Animals.* "Will and reason were powerless." Telling ourselves not to feel fear is like telling ourselves not to blink when we sneeze. Our bodies know what they know, and trying to fight that programming is a waste of time. What really matters most is how we use our conscious minds to handle that knowledge.

That means, in essence, not responding to fear unthinkingly, as our bodies are apt to do. Because the kinds of fears we face today rarely require the type of fast action we need to flee a saber-toothed tiger, we need to listen to our fear reaction without acting mindlessly or allowing ourselves to be paralyzed. In cases where we allow our fear to overcome our rational thought, it can lead to inaction, which may be an inappropriate response, or lead us to actions that are irrational, illogical, and what we would probably call stupid, all in a misguided attempt to protect ourselves. Sometimes in fear-based situations, such as being afraid of getting caught having made a serious error, we lie or go to extreme lengths in order to cover the initial blunder. As we scramble in fear to find a solution, we end up losing sight of the bigger picture and often make things worse. We over-respond to a perceived threat, one that may be better resolved through thought and measured action, rather than a quick reaction.

I deal with this all the time with my clients. In a crisis situation, fear makes everything worse. It is one of those emotions that most often drive us to ruinous decisions. Fear can cause us to become delusional, it can plunge us deeper into a state of denial, and it can cause us to lie in order to avoid the perceived consequences, thus compounding the initial problem. In a crisis situation when fear is amplified, many people have a knee-jerk reaction to reestablish short-term control, but when it comes to dealing with fear, you have to think both short- and long-term. The instinct to want to regain control is not a bad one, but it's far better to step back, assess the larger picture, and act accordingly, even if this opens you up to criticism in the short term. I tell my clients that it is better to accept that they messed up and trust that this is the best way to deal with the problem no matter how uncomfortable it is.

It's not about trying to control the amount of fear we experience or trying not to feel fear at all; that's not possible. Instead, learning how to deal with fear—to listen to it—is what makes the difference between a positive or disastrous outcome. The art of fear management is about figuring out what to do with that fear when it arises. Much as with anger, we must learn to cope with it in a way that is not ultimately detrimental to us. More often than not we should accept our fear and measure the impact of it on us, then seek to find a rational response to it.

Unhealthy Fear: When Fear Hurts Us

There are as many things people fear as there are people, and any one or combination of them can lead to crisis, especially if the fear isn't recognized and handled in a prudent manner. This book would be as thick as a phone book if I tried to list all the fears people have and how things could go awry, so I will discuss a few common ones that I have seen in my work; many of the ideas in these examples can be applied to almost any kind of fear.

Fear Factor 1: The Fear of Getting Caught

This is the biggie. We all make mistakes, of course, but the thought of what could happen or what people would think if we were found out can be terrifying. In Washington, there is a saying: The cover-up is worse than the crime. It's an easy trap to fall into when you begin to realize that something embarrassing, damaging, or unsavory is about to happen. But think about it: How many scandals are made worse because someone tried to hide the truth? I can tell you from experience there are a lot of them. Take Anthony Weiner, whom we discussed in a previous chapter. He eventually lost his position in Congress due to texting unsolicited pictures of himself in his underwear to several women. When the story first broke, his first response, no doubt grounded in fear, was to deny that he had sent or even taken the pictures. Then he said that someone might have hacked into his phone. Did any of us think he was telling the truth, except possibly his mother?

Yet Weiner's fear of being exposed, having to tell his wife

and suffer public humiliation, got the better of him and he kept lying. Each time he put himself in a worse position, possibly compounding his fear, because with each lie he had more to answer for. I think it's possible that if Weiner had immediately owned up to his stupid move, rather than teasing the media and dragging the story out with each unlikely excuse, there might have been one blast of bad publicity from which he could have recovered. Instead, he was so afraid of the consequences of telling the truth that he made the story much worse. His fear of the repercussions wound up ensuring that his career wouldn't survive. Had he been more in tune with these fears to begin with, maybe he never would have sent out the pictures in the first place.

Weiner is an example of what happens when fear dominates our actions. It might be one of the other characteristics in this book, such as ego or denial, that gets us into trouble to begin with. But being dominated by fear is what ultimately compounds the crisis and can lead to even greater consequences.

Fear Factor 2: Fear of Change

Fear of change can best be exemplified by the story of a man who couldn't face up to the fact that his decades-long job as a TV executive was over and it was time to move on. He'd been at the network in one position or another for the bulk of his forty-year career and had worked his way up. The board was in the midst of transitioning him because it "was taking the programming in a new direction," which is a rather polite way of saying that he would soon be fired. I spoke to him about how to message his transition and how to choose an exit date. Although he accepted the board's decision, he was uncooperative and began to stonewall the board, withholding information and hanging on to projects. It became obvious to me that he was acting stubbornly in his approach mainly because of fear. This place was all he knew; he had invested time and energy in this position and it represented a part of his identity that was now being threatened. A threat to someone's very sense of self is profoundly difficult to face. He was afraid of what would happen to him once his tenure was over.

His concern wasn't necessarily practical; this guy had great credentials, and he was qualified to find another job—at a cable network, in academia, or at a production company—very easily. I reminded him that this was the end of a chapter, not the end of everything. But he was so afraid of the unknown that he wasn't able to see that there were plenty of great opportunities within his reach. He could very easily have gone on to do any number of things, but his fear of leaving the comfort zone of his position with the network blinded him.

While his actions did delay his departure somewhat, they also hurt his reputation both inside and outside the company, which ultimately made it more difficult for him to find a satisfactory position. Trying to regain a lost reputation, especially at an advanced stage of your career, can be next to impossible. I'm not saying that he was in an easy position—it's hard to find yourself being asked to leave a place that's comfortable, especially when your sense of identity is wrapped up in that place and job. But if he had been able to look beyond the bad news of having to make a life change, he would have seen that he actually still had a lot of interesting options. Instead he chose actions that only made it worse for him in the long run.

Fear Factor 3: Fear of Failure

Of course, you don't have to be in the middle of a full-fledged crisis to have problems with fear. It can be a constant, low-level hum in your life that keeps you from standing up for yourself or going after your dreams. Coupled with anxiety, fear frequently comes not from some external source but from our own insecurities and self-doubt. Fear can keep you from asking out an attractive person you meet on the train. It can keep you from buying a dress you love and will look good in because you fear others' perceptions that you're trying to look too young. It can keep you from advocating for yourself in the office for fear of getting a reputation as a troublemaker. Some of us have big, identifiable fears, sometimes vestiges from the way we were raised (such as a fear of having to do without, if we were raised poor), but most of the time we don't even know what we're afraid of. The fear—low-grade, constant fear as well as sharper fear—resides within us and causes us to engage in a cycle of poor decisions that only affirm our fears more.

Take Pat, for example, who knew from the time she was in elementary school that she would grow up to be a lawyer. This wasn't just a whimsical dream of a young girl but the determined conviction of someone who would grow up to be the fifth generation of her family to attend law school. She excelled in her coursework and graduated at the top of her class. After graduation, as expected, she landed a job at one of Boston's top law firms. Along with all the other first-years, Pat took the bar exam. Like many of them, she failed.

This shouldn't be something to be ashamed of. Some estimates hold that 50 to 70 percent of people fail the exam the first time. Undeterred, albeit a little shaken, she tried again. Again (this time along with three other associates at her firm) she was unsuccessful. She tried a third time with the same result. She was now the only person left from her cohort who had not secured a passing mark. A lifelong dream and expectation of practicing law was quickly and quite simply becoming just that—a dream. Pat was deeply ashamed.

Pat was riddled with very real and daunting fears. Her bosses felt that she was a brilliant associate with the potential to go far. It was just a matter of passing this exam, and she didn't test well. If she took the test and failed, again, how would she cope with the embarrassment? How would she respond to the whispers and gossip of former classmates and colleagues who surely were judging her? How would she deal with not being able to live up to her family legacy? On a rational level, Pat knew that it was just a test, and that the test was no reflection of her abilities as a lawyer—her excellent work at the firm so far and her coursework proved that. Still, she was scared and instead of honestly tackling and dealing with these problems, she made the difficult decision to leave the firm and gave up on her dream of being a lawyer. She left behind a career that she had envisioned having since she was a child because she couldn't bring herself to face the embarrassment of failing the bar exam one more time.

Pat was fortunate to have family money and a husband who earned a good salary, so she was still able to live a comfortable lifestyle. This wouldn't have been problematic if she was truly OK with not practicing law, but she grieved for her lost career. I sometimes wonder whether if Pat had had no other options, no financial security to fall back on, things would have turned out differently for her. In this case, the comfort of having a Plan B allowed her to bypass her fears and avoid the discomfort of having to risk failure again.

Fear Factor 4: Fear of Losing Status

For most of us, too much fear is far more common than too little. Maybe I'm projecting, based on my own charge-ahead, march-to-your-own-drummer-even-if-it-makes-you-unpopular personality, but for me, being held back by fear is the saddest thing in the world. Taking risks can lead to wonderful things. There are adventures and interesting people around every corner. If you let fear get in the way of living life or reacting to it, you prevent yourself from doing all the things you want to do.

Carol Dweck, a professor of psychology at Stanford University, has spent much of her career studying children who, for various reasons, are afraid to take risks for fear of looking stupid or failing. Whether because of the messages they've received at home or a certain level of caution they were born with, these kids believe that being smart means never making a mistake. In her book *Mindset: The New Psychology of Success,* Dweck discusses two ways of looking at the world that can have an impact on how risk-averse people are. Dweck suggests that children whose intelligence was overpraised may be led to believe success is based on innate ability—that you are as smart or capable as you are and there's nothing much you can do to change that. Children with this fixed view of intelligence are often afraid to stretch themselves or try something that might be hard because they can only lose: they're afraid that if they fail, they won't be seen as smart anymore, and they believe that's a highly valued trait.

If you think your skills are what they are and can't be improved upon, you have no incentive to try again after a failure. You're too afraid. As these children grow into adults and enter the workforce, they most likely will settle for safe jobs rather than take a risk on something outside their comfort zone. This can eventually lead to dissatisfaction and boredom as the tasks they choose for themselves present insufficient stimulation. Those of us who have less of a stake in failure—who either believe that there's room for improvement so why not try, or who don't care as much how they're perceived—have less of this kind of fear.

Fear Factor 5: Fear of a Secret Being Uncovered

We all sometimes fear what others will think if they know the "real" us. This type of fear is common and often leads to needless crises. Here is an example of how getting out in front of a fear is the best way to handle a crisis, rather than caving in to it.

Actor Neil Patrick Harris is an example of someone who was able to weigh his fears against his situation and come out on top. In 2006, Harris, who is gay but was not public about it at that time, got word that he was about to be outed by a gossip blog. In fact, he was playing a horn-dog hetero frat-boy type on *How I Met Your Mother*, and this revelation, he had reason to fear, might affect his career. Harris had to make a decision about how to handle the impending situation: Should he take action and comment on his sexuality or do nothing and hope the story didn't get too big? Both options involved a certain degree of fear.

Harris probably felt that he had to take the risk to head off the impending witch hunt. So he jumped in front of the story and came out to *People* magazine. Harris thus avoided being put in the defensive position of having to react to the news rather than setting the tone himself. That took bravery. While he was already out to his family and friends and had a longtime partner, he came out to everyone "and sort of squashed the fires." The response was . . . nada. Barely a blip. It was brilliantly handled because whatever fear Harris might have had about the public perception and effect on his career was weighed against the alternative. "The last thing you want to do is talk about your private life based on scandal," Harris explained to Ellen DeGeneres on her talk show in 2007. And although he must have wrestled with the decision, the out-come was completely in his favor. Harris continues to work on his TV show and play a frat-boy type both on his show and in the *Harold & Kumar* movies. He hosted the Tony Awards to great acclaim in 2011 (and even had fun with stereotypes about homosexuality and musical theater). His career is going stronger than ever. And having faced down his fear, his identity can't be used against him anymore.

Fear Factor 6: Fear of Physical or Emotional Repercussions

The most heartbreaking kind of fear of all is the fear carried by a person in an abusive relationship. It's easy for an outsider to ask, "Why didn't she just leave?" But the fear in the heart of an abused person of what will happen if she does is unfathomable to anyone who hasn't experienced it.

There are many theories that attempt to explain why people stay in abusive relationships (both men and women can be the abused or the abuser), and I don't want to try and simplify a very complicated matter in these pages. I do want to, however, briefly discuss a well-known model that I believe can help you see how such fear is cultivated by the abuser over months and years, and why it's so hard for the person on the receiving end to overcome. It can and must be overcome, however; and when the abused person starts to see the pattern of what's taking place, she finds her own power and amasses the outside support to change her seemingly hopeless situation.

In her book *The Battered Woman*, Dr. Lenore Walker delineates three phases of abuse: the tension-building phase, the crisis phase where the abuse occurs (although I would argue that the first phase is another form of abuse), and the reconciliation or honeymoon phase. The first builds a rock-solid foundation for the fear, the second realizes it, and the third serves to convince the abused person that there's another side to her abuser, one that will prevail if only she behaves well enough. Of course, whether or not the abuser chooses to abuse has nothing to do with how "good" the abused person is.

In the first phase, the tension phase, the abused is dominated by the fear of "setting off" his or her partner's volatile nature. The abuser is moody, critical, and emotionally manipulative, nitpicking at his partner's faults, is sullen and withdrawn, and may even openly mock or verbally abuse her. To keep from triggering her partner's anger, she will walk on eggshells, trying anything to keep the situation calm and the abuser happy, including watching what she says and wears, whom she talks to, and staying away from people he doesn't like (usually those who see what's going on). During this phase, the fear of what will happen if the abuser becomes unhinged is so great that it colors everything the abused person does. It forces her to accommodate, often doing exactly what her partner says he wants, no matter how inconvenient or unreasonable it may be.

Inevitably, though, something goes wrong—something is said or done that inexplicably infuriates the abuser—moving the cycle into the crisis phase. The abused may feel she's at fault for setting him off. That's when the physical or emotional violence occurs, and the abused moves to protect herself and may even call the police, file a restraining order, or decide to leave. The fear is so great in the moment that concern about her short-term well-being takes precedence. This action prompts the abuser to apologize, beg for forgiveness, offer to go to counseling, and promise to "never do it again." Sadly, more often than not, the abused sees potential for the way things could be.

Abusers can be very convincing, and things may even temporarily improve as the abuser is on his best behavior (the "honeymoon phase"). But that's not the only reason abused women stay. She may be financially dependent on her abuser, or worry what others will think of her leaving after she's defended him for so long. Mostly, she has hope that this time will be different, that he'll be better. She just wants things to be the way she believes they could be, and that he's claiming they can. But because of the cyclical nature of chronic abuse, eventually old behaviors return and they cycle back to the tension-building phase where the abused is once again dominated and controlled by fear.

This model suggests that fear is a primary motivator for those who stay in abusive relationships, but you'll notice that fear motivates different responses. In the tension-building phase, fear motivates the abused to try to contain the crisis, to control the situation by conforming. In the crisis phase, however, fear motivates a more positive action—to leave or press charges. If enough momentum can be sustained in this second phase, and if the abused can garner enough support for her decision, often this survivalist fear can result in a happier outcome than returning for another round of psychological and possibly physical violence. Professional counseling is often necessary for the abused to recognize the cycle—and learn how to listen to her fear—and end it before it begins again.

If you are in such a cycle or know someone who is, recognizing the role fear plays will help to end it. The abused fears the response of the abuser, but also has some internal fears that are holding her hostage, typically fear of loneliness, fear that she'll do no better with the next person, and perhaps financial fears. Help that person imagine what life would be like when she's free from the control of someone else. Finding the courage to use your fear positively—to listen to it and choose an affirmative action to change your situation, rather than simply obey the fear and try to contain it—will ultimately get you out from under.

Managing Fear: Taking the Risk

In order to want to face your fears—which is tremendously difficult to do, but offers great reward—the reward has to be something so desirable, so stress-relieving, or so life-improving that it makes the unpleasantness of walking through the fire of fear worth it.

Neil Patrick Harris overcame his fear of people's opinions of his sexuality, it seems, in order to feel more in control of his situation, which was worth it to him. "Without fear, there would be no need for bravery," Jeff Wise writes in *Extreme Fear*. It's true. Being afraid is an opportunity for testing ourselves and becoming proud of ourselves, which is exhilarating and leads to a reduction in fear overall. I think the key to courage is thinking about the energy you waste being afraid: Facing the source of that anxiety may trigger a burst of distress, but it may also end the distress you've been feeling for so long. It means you won't keep wasting energy with fear and making decisions that don't further your success or happiness based on that fear. There may be undesirable consequences in the short term—you've been avoiding experiencing this fear because it's not pleasant to do so—but there's also the opportunity for you to get feelings off your chest, improve a situation that's been troubling you, and feel empowered by facing your fear.

While fear may seem to present insurmountable obstacles, once we embrace it, it can sometimes force us to move ahead; if we can bear the constant anxiety it brings us to carry out a plan we believe in, it can often create spectacular results. In fact, the experience of having failed can often give you a "what have I got to lose?" attitude that can lead you to take risks unburdened by the fear of failing.

J. K. Rowling, the creator of Harry Potter, is a great example of this. She once said, "I've often met people who are terrified, in a straitjacket of their own making, because they'd rather do anything than fail." Rowling knows what it's like to live with the fear of not being able to make ends meet; she was once a single mother struggling to support her child while she worked on her first Harry Potter novel in an Edinburgh café. Around the time that she began writing, her mother passed away, her short marriage fell apart, and she was diagnosed with depression. If anyone would be likely to fear failure, it would be a first-time novelist who had no evidence that she could succeed. She had already "failed," however, which she alluded to in a commencement address she later gave at Harvard, and so perhaps felt she had little to lose. Yet she sat in that café day after day while her daughter slept beside her.

Rowling's finished manuscript (typed up on an old manual typewriter) was rejected by twelve publishers before finally Bloomsbury paid 1,500 British pounds (about 2,500 American dollars) for it.

Today, Rowling is a billionaire who does loads of charity work. But once upon a time, she was a frightened young mom with a failed marriage who had to move to live near her sister because she had no other family or prospects. She could have tried to get a safer, more predictable source of income, and had she let a fear of failure get in her way, she would not have chased her dream. Yet fear didn't stop her.

An excerpt from a commencement address that Rowling delivered at Harvard University was featured in a 2008 *New York Times* article entitled "The Best Commencement Speeches Ever." Rowling speaks on the connection between success and failure:

> Failure meant the stripping away of the inessential. I stopped pretending to myself that I was anything other than what I was, and began directing all my energy into finishing the only work that mattered to me. Had I really succeeded in anything else, I might never have found the determination to succeed in the one arena where I found I truly belonged. I was set free, because my greatest fear had been realized, and I was

still alive, and I still had a daughter whom I adored, and I had an old typewriter, and a big idea. And so rock bottom became the solid foundation on which I rebuilt my life. You might never fail on the scale I did, but some failure in life is inevitable. It is impossible to live without failing at something, unless you live so cautiously that you might as well not have lived at all—in which case, you fail by default.

One of the big motivators to overcome fear is doing the right thing and helping others, but those instances are rare enough that they are still remarkable. So powerful is fear that even when motivated by what we consider right, most of us will not step up to the plate. In *The Social Animal: The Hidden Sources of Love, Character, and Achievement,* David Brooks cites a Penn State study showing that while half of students surveyed said they would protest if someone made a sexist comment in their presence, only 16 percent actually did (after the researchers arranged for it to happen). It takes real courage to speak up, to go against the social grain, to shatter norms.

Some of the bravest fear-facers have been whistle-blowers. The pioneering investigative journalist Nellie Bly actually put her life at risk to expose wrongdoing. As a teenager, she talked her way into a newspaper gig to help support her family. She first went undercover in the 1880s, writing about the plight of the poor young girls who worked in New York City's sweatshops, back when young women didn't often have careers. When clothing manufacturers threatened an advertising boycott because of her columns, Bly's editors tried to move her over to the society pages. Fed up, she took herself to Mexico at twenty-one and covered abuses there and got kicked out of the country. She then got herself an assignment at Joseph Pulitzer's paper *The World* in New York, infiltrating the Women's Lunatic Asylum on Blackwell's Island in the East River. She acted crazy in public and got herself arrested, then in the courtroom claimed to have amnesia. She was declared insane by several doctors and committed to the madhouse.

She must have been terrified, but she memorized all she experienced so that she could write an exposé about it when she got out: She and her fellow patients were given scraps of dried bread, rancid butter, and filthy water. Human waste and rats were everywhere. The nurses beat the patients and poured freezing water over their heads. Talking to her fellow inmates, Bly became convinced that some were completely sane. In her book *Ten Days in a Mad-House* (1887), she wrote:

> What, excepting torture, would produce insanity quicker than this treatment? . . . I would like the expert physicians who are condemning me for my action, which has proven their ability, to take a perfectly sane and healthy woman, shut her up and make her sit from 6 a.m. until 8 p.m. on straight-back benches, do not allow her to talk or move during these hours, give her no reading and let her know nothing of the world or its doings, give her bad food and harsh treatment, and see how long it will take to make her insane. Two months would make her a mental and physical wreck.

The newspaper for which she was working arranged her release, and her reporting made her a sensation. The asylum was investigated by a grand jury and ordered to make the improvements Bly recommended. She went on to investigate corrupt lobbyists, the treatment of women prisoners by the police, the failures of health care for the poor, and the experiences of railway workers during the Pullman railroad strike in 1894.

While Nellie Bly was before my time, it's safe to conclude that she faced fears that would and no doubt did paralyze lesser men and women. There's a chance that she was simply braver than the average person and thus didn't need to work as hard to overcome her fears, but more likely she was particularly good at managing her fears so they didn't stop her from doing what she felt she had to do.

Many brave people who speak out against injustice suffer for their truth telling but choose to follow their consciences anyway. The abuses at Abu Ghraib prison might never have come to light if it weren't for the ethics of Joe Darby, a soldier at Abu Ghraib. When one of his colleagues gave him a disc of photos depicting the torture of Arab prisoners, he agonized over what to do. Despite the personal risks to his career, Darby pushed through the fear of what could happen and slipped a copy of the CD under the door of the army's Criminal Investigation Command late at night. He'd been a friend of some of the soldiers whose deplorable acts were depicted on the discs, but he couldn't ignore what he'd seen. He'd wanted anonymity—an indication of the fear of retaliation he no doubt felt—but his identity was discovered, leading to a hailstorm of abuse. His home was vandalized, other military families stopped speaking to him and his family, and his life was threatened. He and his wife had to go into protective custody at an undisclosed location.

To outsiders, it may appear that doing the right thing only led to heartache and scorn. However, surprisingly, Darby does not regret his choice because he firmly believed that he was on the right side morally, and he must feel good about not letting fear stop him from doing what he knew was right. In a 2006 *GQ* interview he stated:

> I don't regret any of it. I made my peace with my decision before I turned the pictures in. I knew that if people found out it was me, I wouldn't be liked. That's why I wanted to be anonymous. I knew what the mentality is up there . . . [But] I never doubted that it was the right thing. It forced a big change in my life, [and] the change has been good and bad. I liked my little quiet town, but now I have a new place, with a new job and new opportunities. And I'm going to live my life like anyone else, and raise my family.

The bottom line is, managing your fear involves taking a clear look at what is to be gained by taking a risk and what is to be lost, and whether or not that's worth it to you. The payoff in terms of helping others or doing what you know you have to do to live without regret must be weighed against any risk to your well-being.

But weighing this risk is critical, and people who fail to do this are often not in touch with the healthy fear that might save them personal injury. Witness my own careless behavior of a few years ago. I was in New York with my friend for the weekend. I had just returned from a trip to Egypt and was proudly wearing my most cherished souvenir, a beautiful 22-karat gold necklace. My friend Robin and I were walking out of a sandwich shop as she was intently explaining to me the difference between the taste of fountain Coke and bottled Coke. In the middle of her impassioned analysis, a stranger suddenly approached me from behind, yanked my necklace from around my neck, and ran off.

Without thinking I took off after him. Anger overcame me and I chased him for ten blocks—waving my arms and screaming for the people I pushed past on the crowded streets to call the police. I was yelling at him, assuring him that when I caught him I was going to beat him to a pulp (despite the fact that I'm a relatively small woman and with his stature he could have been a linebacker for the New York Giants). But after realizing that I wasn't giving up and was determined to make the biggest scene possible, he finally dropped the necklace before he entered Central Park.

It worked out, but in retrospect, I wish I had felt more fear, or listened to the whisper of fear that must have been trying to be heard. Not once did it occur to me not to go after him. As I was speaking to the police, they pointed out that I put my life at risk by chasing someone who could have had a gun or a knife. I never really thought through what would happen if I actually did catch him—as the adrenaline pumped through my blood, I just acted without thinking.

At that point, my priority was solely my necklace and not my safety. I failed to weigh the consequences, which could have gotten me hurt or worse.

When we call people fearless, we're usually responding to a combination of other qualities they have—determination, decisiveness, optimism, bravery, and any number of other traits—not thoughtless actions. Nelly Bly seems to have been a good example of this. The other qualities she had clearly took precedence over any fear she might have felt in fighting injustice with her pen. What we often call fearlessness is more likely a lot of confidence blended with a lot of smart preparation.

Taking Baby Steps

At this point it's clear that there's such a thing as a healthy amount of fear, which keeps you safe, and a reasoned reaction to even a terrible fear, which might result in a smarter outcome than a rash reaction would. So, how do we shift the problematic concept of fear from something we avoid at all costs to something that can play a valuable, balanced part in our lives? How do we use fear to stop us from making foolish mistakes and push us to make wiser decisions? How can we use our fear as motivation to achieve rather than as a justification for failure? We all are capable of meeting our greatest fears head-on, so long as we have the tools to do so.

The first thing I recommend is breaking your fear down into smaller components, each of which is more easily overcome, rather than thinking about it as a huge, overwhelming blob that could consume your life. Procrastinators are famous for doing the latter—procrastination is simply fear of failure in disguise. Noted sociologist Erving Goffman believed that people who are fearful but don't recognize fear as their primary problem often engage in a "series of preventative strategies" to avoid facing the fear. Perfectionists tend to procrastinate because they see their goals as terrifying and impossible. They tell themselves, "Why bother starting? I'm going to fail." The fear of never reaching their goals, of failing, prevents them from approaching them fully. But we can often talk ourselves into baby steps.

If you're having problems with your spouse you don't have to think about changing your entire relationship in one sitting; that is too overwhelming and will keep you rooted in your fear and unlikely to face it. But you can applaud yourself for simply broaching the subject of the socks on the floor or your desire to feel more supported in your career—call that a success, because it is. If you have big career goals that require more schooling, you don't have to give up on them because you're afraid that you'll never be able to do all it takes to get into Yale; you can take one night-school course and go from there. Perfectionism may not look like fear, but that's often what it is.

Anne Lamott wrote a famous guide to writing called *Bird by Bird*—the title came from her father's advice to her brother, who'd left his big ornithology report until the last second and was facing a huge pile of profiles of birds to write. "Just take it bird by bird," Lamott's father said. That's all any of us can do with our fears—tackle them bird by bird. If you're honest about what you want and what fears are preventing you from getting it, you can take one small step toward it.

Just Doing It

Sometimes, just powering through your fear can help. This is the principle behind aversion therapy, which psychologists often use to help people with phobias, or extreme fears, overcome them. While some advocate complete immersion in that which you fear, in order to desensitize yourself to it, most experts favor a more moderate, gradual approach of exposing yourself to that which you fear and realizing that you can handle it better than you think you can. Over time, you build the confidence that turns the fear into something you notice, perhaps, but that doesn't have a strong influence over the way you respond to a situation.

The way my mom overcame a terrible fear she had is a good example of this. She was in a horrific car accident many years ago. A child darted out from between parked cars into the street and she hit her. She was absolutely devastated; for almost two years after that, she was too scared to drive a car, and no amount of pleading by my father or anyone else could change her mind. But eventually, she decided to face her fears. She agreed to be a passenger. My dad drove slowly around the block while my mom clutched the dashboard, gritting her teeth and breathing fast. Gradually my dad could drive longer and longer distances with my mom, and she relaxed a bit more each time. A few months later, she began driving on her own. She drove incredibly slowly and was so alert she was practically vibrating, but she faced her fears. I was terrifically proud of her for accepting that one upsetting, terrible accident in a car did not mean that she had to cut herself off from driving entirely.

Reappraise and Talk Yourself Down

There's a psychological term, "self-efficacy," that basically means "feeling like you can handle whatever comes along." Telling yourself that you, too, can cope like the people mentioned in this chapter may help you manage your fear when you're in a difficult situation. Not being ruled by fear does not mean not feeling it. It may mean simply noticing that you feel fear, but you don't have to act on it, just like you presumably don't act on every physical attraction you feel or eat every delicious piece of chocolate cake that you come across. Psychologists call this "self-regulation," and we use it all the time to keep our emotions in line.

Sure, sometimes self-regulation doesn't work. We overspend, we overeat, we overreact. But most of the time, most of us tend to self-regulate pretty well without even realizing it. And when we feel in control, we have a better chance to make good choices, fulfill our commitments, and get things done. When you are faced with a fear, it can be helpful to remind yourself that you self-regulate successfully all the time, and there's no reason you can't in this instance as well. It's when we feel that we don't have control over our lives that fear and other emotions can crush us. We get depressed and stressed. In *Extreme Fear,* author Jeff Wise discusses a series of laboratory experiments determining that subjects are less bothered by electric shocks when they believe that they have some control over them. In other words, if we're prepared for what's coming, that confers a sense of control and we're far more able to cope.

Performing what scientists call a "reappraisal" can also cut your fears down to size in a hurry. Let's say a crisis is starting to play around the edges of your reality. Maybe it's a disaster at work; maybe it's a personal issue that's starting to spin out of control. First, take a few deep breaths. Then take a mental step back and try to shift from a negative point of view ("I'm terrified, everything is going to hell in a handbasket") to a more objective one ("If others were telling me about this crisis in their lives, here are the issues I would tell them to be aware of; here are consequences that could occur; here are the steps I would tell them to take to try to get things back on track"). Scientists say that reinterpreting a situation in a positive or even neutral way can help you manage fear.

Remember, too, that the anticipation of consequences can often be worse than whatever it is you actually feared in the first place. Seymour Epstein, a psychologist at the University of Massachusetts–Amherst, conducted a study in which novice skydivers wore heart-rate monitors. Their pulses raced faster and faster as the plane rose, right until the moment they stepped out of the plane. Then their heart rates slowed dramatically when they took the leap. That's a dramatic example, but it's true of so much of what we fear—anticipating the experience is the worst part and we usually exaggerate how scary the outcome will be.

Managing Others' Fear

Much of this chapter is about personal fear and how caving to that fear can lead to crisis—crises that take a certain amount of fearlessness to face down. Sometimes, though, we are called upon to manage crises that create fear in others. Taking a look at how leaders, both in government and in the private sector, effectively manage crises of fear can be very helpful in understanding how to manage our own.

Consider, for example, the actions of Rudy Giuliani in the period following the attacks on the World Trade Center towers. He for the most part employed the POWER model, without, of course, knowing that's what he was doing.

Giuliani was tasked with the challenge of managing not only his fears but that of a populace in a way few other politicians have been able to do. People of all political persuasions were moved by the mayor's words and presence. He slept only two hours the night of September 11 and the next day met with a psychologist who worked as a consultant for the city's school system. According to the *New York Times*, the psychologist told him, "Speak with an authoritative voice and never promise more safety than you can deliver; voice your anger, but direct it at the real enemy." The psychologist told the *Times* that he'd advised Giuliani to be honest above all else. "You say, 'We're safe'—well, how do we know that? Make clear the steps to safety."

Despite any criticism leveled against him for other things he did during his terms as mayor, his legacy will be that of a heroic politician who restored hope and unity to a broken city. Before the attacks, many New Yorkers loathed Giuliani.

His approval rating the previous year was at 36 percent. Six weeks after 9/11, his rating was 79 percent. While it's not fair or accurate to say that one enormous right move can override several smaller wrong moves, there's no debating the fact that Giuliani's extraordinary strength under pressure will endure as a major legacy of his political career.

What he did do right was take what seemed to be an uncontrollable event that struck fear in the hearts of millions of people and reframe it in a way that was more manageable and even less scary to those involved. Using our POWER model we can examine how he successfully navigated this crisis. He *pinpointed* the fear and devastation the attacks had brought and addressed these feelings head-on, and was straightforward with information at a time when the city was being besieged by rumored reports of additional attacks and threats. He *owned* his own emotions, thereby enabling people to own the fear by not hiding his own shock and horror, but at the same time encouraged them to work through what was going on. He helped to empower them with concrete guidance that could potentially thwart another attack, which was *working it through*. If something seemed off, if their instincts were telling them that someone or something should not be trusted, he challenged New Yorkers to be proactive and contact the authorities, which gave many people more of a sense of control. Giuliani also helped *explore* everyone's worst fear—another attack. He assured residents that resources and plans were in place even if the city was hit again. By treating the crisis honestly and openly, he was able to transform fear from a paralyzing emotion into an actionable plan.

But his handling of the crisis was not without criticism. Giuliani was nearing the end of his second term as mayor of New York City and even though he had previously pushed for term limits, he now was proposing that they should be overturned in order to "maintain the unity that exists in the city." A Quinnipiac poll showed that over 55 percent of NYC voters did not want an extension of Giuliani's tenure. One of the criticisms launched against Giuliani is that while his actions and leadership rallied New Yorkers together as never before, he later was seen by some as stoking that fear and taking advantage of the political capital that 9/11 afforded him. If you agree with this assessment of his behavior, it would seem as though he failed to enact the last stage of the POWER model and never reestablished a sense of balance or *reined in* his crisis-mode behavior. All things considered, though, Giuliani emerged out of a fearful situation as a well-respected leader and joined the ranks of some of the most revered politicians in modern history.

Another example of POWER in action is the way a company, Johnson & Johnson, handled a crisis in 1982. The company's product Tylenol has instant brand recognition and Johnson & Johnson is often rated as one of the most well-respected companies in the world. Not many people associate the company with a tragic crisis that took the lives of seven people.

A twelve-year-old girl in Chicago died that fall after taking a capsule of Extra Strength Tylenol. Shortly afterward six other people died too; three of these people were members of the same family. It was quickly discovered that the common thread in these deaths was the over-the-counter pain reliever Tylenol. Investigators soon discovered that the bottles had been tampered with and the pills were laced with cyanide.

It did not take long for these murders to saturate the national headlines. Suddenly a spotlight was brightly focused not only on Tylenol products, but also on the larger issue of pharmaceutical safety. Johnson & Johnson was faced with the challenge of reestablishing trust in its products by assuaging fears that this could happen again.

This case is widely considered the gold standard for crisis management—and for good reason. The response was quick, effective, and transparent. Most importantly, the company was able to break through the culture of fear and reestablish trust with its customers through a proactive campaign. In her book *Crisis Communications: A Casebook Approach,* Kathleen Fearn-Banks details the manner in which Johnson & Johnson handled the tainted-drug crisis three decades ago. First the company's team *pinpointed* the emotion that they were going to have to address, which, of course, in this case was the fear that a trusted product meant to relieve pain could, instead, cause death. They then had to *own* the fact that while this tampering could have happened to any product, it had happened to their product. Because of this, they were fully aware that it had become their responsibility to redefine standards of product safety since the nation would be judging their actions in the days, weeks, months, and years to come. They also had to do an enormous amount of work. For example, while the FBI and FDA advised against a complete recall (as they saw it as a surrender to an act of potential terrorism), Johnson & Johnson recalled over twenty-five million bottles of their product. It was a drastic, costly measure, but the company believed that this was the appropriate action given the potential risk to consumers.

Over and over again, they took strong steps (*working it through*) to make clear that they were doing everything possible to get to the bottom of the crisis and to put new measures in place to keep the unthinkable from happening again. They also *explored* ways to prevent this in the future by re-launching Tylenol with a triple-seal tamper-resistant bottle. Finally they *reined in* the fears of the public by appealing to the relationship that had already been established between the company and its customers. They created a toll-free number for customers to call if they wanted information about the product recalls; they distributed coupons to encourage customers to purchase the re-launched products. They launched an advertising campaign that openly explained what happened and the steps they were taking to prevent it from happening again. They warned hospitals nationwide about the potential for contaminated containers and established transparent lines of communication with the press. The press, in turn, was largely supportive of Johnson & Johnson and praised its efforts to overcome the crisis that ultimately cost the company over one hundred million dollars.

Applying the POWER Model

Are you managing your fear appropriately? Remember, you don't have to be perfectly brave. You just have to find a middle ground between being held back by anxiety and charging ahead too recklessly.

Pinpoint the core trait: In this case, fear.
Own it: Acknowledge that it can be both good and bad.
Work it through: Process the role it has played in your life.
Explore it: Consider how it could play out in the future.
Rein it in: Establish how to re-achieve balance and control.

PINPOINT: The core trait that we're discussing is, of course, fear. Pinpointing it in your daily life might take a bit of detective work because fear can masquerade as perfectionism, apathy (fear of investing too much in something important), and even love (sometimes what a parent, for instance, thinks is love for a child is really fear of losing that child or of not being as important to that child).

OWN IT: You can own your fear by considering how a lack of fear can send you out unprepared into the world, cause conflicts, and trigger bad judgment. Also consider how too much fear, on the other hand, can paralyze you. Remind yourself that fear is normal, healthy, and adaptive as long as you don't let it box you in.

WORK IT THROUGH: Consider whether you've let the balance tilt too far and let your fears paralyze you (or, though this is less likely, whether you're not afraid enough, not being realistic about situations in your life).

EXPLORE IT: Figure out what the personal triggers are that make you more likely to lose perspective and panic. Let's say yours is money. If you're a big catastrophizer, you might freak out when your fridge dies because even pondering replacing it makes you think about how broke you are and how you'll never get to buy nice things and everything in your life is horrible and terrifying and you're going to die penniless and alone. Reassess and talk yourself down from these negative assumptions. Instead you can think about another time in the past when you had a financial setback and consider that it did not, in fact, send you to the poorhouse in leg irons. Are you afraid to make changes, to confront others, to put your foot down? Explore how you might learn to diffuse those concerns using the strategies we've discussed in this chapter. Consider managing anxiety by writing down everything you're worried about before you go to bed, then telling yourself you can pick up the piece of paper in the morning. For now, you're going to set it down and give yourself the gift of a good night's sleep. Think about how your life would go if you didn't let fear hold you back.

REIN IT IN: Dial back your fear by taking practical steps to make changes right now. That may mean writing a memo, sitting your spouse down for a conversation, researching whatever it is that scares or entices you so you can turn inchoate anxieties into something manageable. You don't have to kill your fears. You couldn't, anyway. You just have to channel them. And you can.

Whether you are afraid of admitting to an indiscretion, facing an unpleasant reality about your life, or going up against a powerful opponent, remember that no matter what happens you have to keep moving forward. Bad things might happen, but you have to acknowledge your fear of them in order to develop a plan to deal with the consequences. It's important to put your fears in perspective when you find yourself off balance. Don't deny what you're feeling; put it in a more positive light. Like all the many examples found throughout this chapter, reframing and challenging initial reactions is a key part of managing the many fires you will have in life. Take a healthy approach and try to view the situation with the proper perspective. You may well lose this case, this vote, this battle . . . but you will always be able to get back up and fight again.

4.

AMBITION

I WANT IT ALL

When I told the network president that his news anchor, who had been arrested for drunk driving the night before, had more than one previous DUI in the various states he worked in before coming to Philadelphia, he claimed not to have any knowledge of that fact. He knew the man liked to party but it had never interfered with his professional life.

"His Q rating (measure of a television personality's popularity) is off the charts," he lamented. He went on to tell me how it was considered quite a coup for him, the network president, to snag this man to anchor their consistently low-rated nightly news show. He saw it as the key move in trying to restore the once illustrious show's popularity. It was for the good of the company and I imagined if he succeeded it would look pretty good for him too.

Ambition—blind, blonde, or any other kind—is a prized attribute. We need a certain amount of ambition to dream big, and some days, even to get out of bed in the morning. Without ambition where would we be? Presumably on a couch, unbathed, in a rank T-shirt and stretched-out underpants, watching infomercials. Ambition is what motivates us to achieve our goals. If you're reading this book, odds are that you're ambitious about your career. But there are probably other things you want too—recognition, wealth, fulfillment, and love. The stronger your ambition, the greater the drive to achieve these things. It doesn't guarantee that we will get what we want, but without it we don't even try.

Simply aspiring to achieve goals, however, is not enough. J. M. Power once said, "If you want to make your dreams come true, the first thing you have to do is wake up." The difference between a dreamer and someone with ambition is a plan of action—or if not a fleshed-out plan, the drive and energy to begin a plan. You need to be proactive if you want to realize your ambition; you have to set goals for yourself and then meet those goals. You have to be clear about what you want and then come up with an equally clear path for how you're going to go after it. Ambition is driven by affirmative action, not passive envisioning. Winning the lottery, marrying an heiress, or being discovered by a model agent while shopping at the mall are not ambitions; those are fantasies. Ambition has to involve self-development and effort. Otherwise, it's just wishful thinking.

Still, there's no downside to shooting for the stars, even if you never quite get there. Even if we don't always achieve what we're after, studies have shown that we are still better off for trying. A 2010 study by Kansas State University professor of sociology Chardie Baird and Florida State University professor of sociology John Reynolds found that the mere act of setting ambitious goals can have real, positive results even if the goals are not actually met. They coined the term "adaptive resilience" to describe this phenomenon of a subject being proud of the work he or she had put in even if it did not achieve total success. Healthy ambition, these professors seem to have proven, is its own reward.

One of the rewards of ambition, regardless of goal attainment, is that ambition provides life with a sense of purpose and can be a great motivator. In fact, some people who are highly ambitious might have a condition known as hypomania that elevates energy, creativeness, and risk taking, John Gartner, the author of *The Hypomanic Edge,* suggested to ABC News. "It's a temperament that is similar to mania but is milder, and so more functional," said Gartner. "The energy, the confidence, the risk-taking and not needing much sleep are physiological traits that people are born with, and you do see them" in many successful people.

But while a touch of hypomania would be something people would pay good money for, ambition, like the other characteristics we discuss in this book, has a darker side. This dark side emerges when ambition drives you toward your goals at any cost, obliterating your perspective and causing you to make decisions that can be self-destructive, detrimental, or harmful to others. In a less dramatic fashion, ambition can also cause you to overextend yourself by trying to do so much to obtain your goal that it ends up scattering your resources—the classic case of a workaholic who neglects his family. The key to keeping ambition in balance is self-awareness, which is what we will look at in this chapter. We will examine positive, healthy ambition and how it can lead to remarkable outcomes. We will then look at some examples of where ambition has gone awry and the crisis it creates. Finally, we discuss how to balance or keep in balance the ambition that is driving us.

Positive Ambition: Leading the Way

A balanced sense of ambition is about working hard on short-term goals while also planning ahead for long-term goals. As Anna Fels, MD, a psychiatrist who studies ambition, writes, "ambition requires an imagined future that can be worked toward by the development of skills and expertise." To succeed in our ambitions, we have to simultaneously be in the moment and look toward the future, toward the consequences of our actions. We have to constantly be aware of where we are now and what we need to be striving for.

I'm sure you've known of people who have such tunnel vision as they strive toward a far-off ambition, such as becoming partner in a law firm or meeting the right man and settling down, that they are blind to their day-to-day life. They forgo exercise in favor of late nights eating takeout at the office, and their health suffers; or they focus on the marriage aspect of their ambition without looking closely enough at who they're marrying and wind up unhappy. Ambition can indeed be blinding to what's important long-term.

Why are some people really good at balancing the now

and the later in their ambitions for the future and others so bad at it? Stanford University emeritus professor of psychology Philip Zimbardo believes that it's because different people's brains actually have different orientations toward time. Some people have what he calls a "present time orientation" and others a "future time orientation." People with a future orientation are less impulsive, are better planners, and tend to be more tenacious.

In his book *The Time Paradox: The New Psychology of Time That Will Change Your Life*, Zimbardo compares the way present- and future-oriented people solve a maze. The former leapt into the task immediately, their pencils racing down the maze's corridors and around bends, turning around and backtracking when they hit a cul-de-sac. The people with future orientations often did not start drawing immediately. They looked at the end of the maze and backtracked toward the beginning in their minds. When they reached a branching path, they followed it with their eyes before barreling down it with their pencil. The result is that over 80 percent of the folks with future orientations solved the mazes; less than 60 percent of the people with present orientations, who picked up a pencil and started drawing immediately, finished.

Research like this confirms what I've noticed in my practice, namely that it's important to look at the big picture, which means knowing your goals and developing a strategy to get there. That doesn't mean you'll know every detail before you begin, only that you'll keep trying and be willing to adjust as you go.

One man who began thinking ahead at a very early age

was Bill Gates. The fact that he'd be successful was obvious to those who worked with him every day, but the rest of the world was amazed when he was officially declared a billionaire days before his thirty-second birthday—making him, at the time, the youngest self-made billionaire in history. Gates began his path in the eighth grade when he wrote his first computer program, a tic-tac-toe game, at an exclusive preparatory school in Seattle.

By the age of seventeen, he formed his first venture with Paul Allen (cofounder of Microsoft): Traf-O-Data. Gates and Allen thought they could process the information gathered by state and local government to record the number of vehicles that pass on a highway cheaper and faster than local companies mechanically recording it on rolls of paper tape. They made a few thousand dollars off their success there, and Gates began to think about developing software that did not yet exist. Gates went so far as to contact the creators of a new microcomputer and led them to believe that he was already working on a BASIC interpreter for their system. That company's ambition coupled with Gates's led to the start of Microsoft in 1975, when Gates was just twenty years old. Gates's ambition to be a pioneer in personal computing paid off big-time and led to a net worth today of over $59 billion.

When Gates stepped down as the head of Microsoft he recalled, "When Paul Allen and I started Microsoft more than thirty years ago, we had big dreams about software. We had dreamed about the impact it could have. We talked about a computer on every desk and in every home. It's been amazing to see so much of that dream become a reality and to have touched so many lives. I never imagined what an incredible and important company would spring from those original ideas." His ambition to be first to follow his vision did change the life of people and companies in every country in the world.

Gates came from an economically privileged background, and his ambition seems to have been rooted in a fascination with the technology he created and a desire to have an impact on the world. But many ambitious people are driven by the desire to rise out of their past circumstances. This is especially worthy of admiration because it shows that ambition and hard work can prevail over adversity. Take, for example, Sean Combs—better known as P. Diddy or just Diddy.

Combs was raised in a family with a strong work ethic. After his father was murdered, his mom worked at three jobs to provide a good life for Combs and his sister. When he was twelve, Combs lied about his age in order to secure a paper route. He even created an alias so he could make more money managing a second paper route. He also worked part-time at an amusement park. After high school, Combs attended Howard University, where he continued his entrepreneurial ambitions by running an airport shuttle business and selling term papers to students. (Combs was not the first and will not be the last person to demonstrate that ambition can cloud ethical judgment.)

But because Combs's passion was music, he eventually dropped out of college to take an internship at Uptown Records in New York City. It was unpaid and mostly consisted of grunt work, but his discipline and commitment caught the attention of Andre Harrell, his mentor and the founder of Uptown Records. The gamble Combs took by leaving school paid off when he became the youngest director of A & R ("artists and repertoire," the division of a record label responsible for recruiting and cultivating talent). In this position, Combs managed the hit R&B group Jodeci, whose debut album was so successful Combs was made vice president.

It was not all smooth sailing, though. After only two years, Combs was fired. But instead of looking for another job, he decided, at the age of twenty-one, to create his own label. Within two weeks after he left Uptown, Combs created Bad Boy Records and signed the Notorious B.I.G. to his label. Combs's keen acumen propelled his label to new levels of success, and it turned out he had talent as a performer himself. Several years after the formation of Bad Boy Records, Combs recorded his own album, which won him a Grammy.

Combs's rise to the spotlight encountered several setbacks—his work was often criticized, he was a part of several very public feuds with rival rappers, and he underwent additional public scrutiny during a highly publicized trial in which he was accused of aggravated assault (he was found not guilty). In the book *Sean Combs,* author Dale Evva Gelfand wrote that Sean said: "I was always somebody who closed my eyes and dreamed, then opened my eyes and saw what I had to do." Today, Combs is worth an estimated $500 million and runs a billion-dollar empire that includes a clothing line, restaurants, and a reality show that he produced. "I've never been surprised about what happened to me. I've put in hard work to get to this point. It's like when you become a lawyer—if you're bustin' your ass, you're not surprised when you get your degree. I came in to win."

Taking Time for Ambition to Develop

Combs's quote about opening his eyes and seeing what he needed to do is a perfect image for the kind of future-oriented thinking that ambition requires. But not everybody has specific dreams that they even want to close their eyes to picture. That doesn't mean we don't have ambition within us. It's just that we don't all know what we want at an early age and sometimes it takes years for our ambition to find a focus. Until that time, it might look as if you have no ambition at all.

Take Kathleen, a young woman I know from a modest background who struggled to complete college. She attended seven colleges before finally graduating and had numerous jobs in different fields. She wasn't what you'd call a slacker, but neither was she driven. She was a bit aimless. Her parents didn't place high expectations on her, and she never felt that she was particularly good at anything, and so she didn't know where to begin, and took jobs simply to pay the bills. She knew she wanted to make something of her life, but she had no idea what that might be.

What helped Kathleen tap into her ambition and passion was remaining open and aware of how she felt as she went through her days—in other words, she had an acute awareness of whether there was a sense of satisfaction in her day-to-day life. This type of present-day orientation may not look like ambition as we think of it, but can be helpful in figuring out your long-term goals. Paying attention to what makes you happy and fulfilled and meets your needs in the present can help you plot out a plan for the future.

And that's exactly what Kathleen did. It was when she became a medical assistant at a small clinic that she began to formulate an idea. What Kathleen did that most people do not is take an inventory of her life and decide that she wanted to achieve something meaningful by helping people. Encouraged by the doctors and nurses at the clinic, she made the decision to take the first step and enroll in an accelerated nursing program.

Now Kathleen has plans to be an oncology nurse and has set a goal to complete that training within the next two years. For the first time she excelled in all of her classes. Her ambition kicked in and motivated her. After being given some guidance and structure, she became equipped with the tools to achieve her success. It was a long road for Kathleen—the subject matter didn't always come easy—but in June 2012, Kathleen will graduate with honors and will begin her career as a nurse at the clinic where she was mentored and encouraged.

The Consequences of Too Much Ambition

Although ambition itself is a good thing, for people who do achieve great success, the danger of letting ambition get away from them always exists. Too much ambition can lead to recklessness, cheating, taking shortcuts, and desperate acts. It can also get you into the kind of ethical trouble that leads people to call me. Like most everything it's a matter of balance. When we become too focused on our ambition at the expense of everything else we begin to drift into an area that can become extremely precarious for us.

Given that ambition itself is a positive thing, what causes it to go awry? The next part of this chapter will look at what factors, when added to ambition, throw an ambitious person off balance and can lead to crisis.

Explosive Ambition Formula 1: Ego Plus Ambition

One way ambition can cause havoc is when it is combined with an inflated ego. In my experience, ambition comes first, and excessive ego and narcissism soon follow. What I mean by that is that when most people who are ambitious start out, they are forced to rely on their determination, intelligence, and drive to assist them in their journey to reach their goals. However, once they begin to be successful in their ambition, they forget all they had to do to get there (or feel superior for having achieved all that they have) and let their ego get out of control. And as we saw in chapter 1, too much ego can lead to a sense of entitlement and a different sort of blindness to the consequences of our actions. In short, too much ego and ambition is an explosive combination.

Perhaps this is why we see so many politicians, who once started off from humble beginnings and a desire for good, fall victim to a dangerous mix of abundant ambition and ego. Healthy ambition makes a person aim high without losing sight of his or her potential limitations. He or she knows that part of achieving a goal is learning how to use personal strengths and weaknesses to overcome those limitations.

The problem is, ego enters into the equation when the success of achieving the goal becomes a heady experience, and in the mind of the aspiring person (and often the minds of others) *the fact* that the person has achieved the ambition becomes evidence of his or her greatness, not how hard he worked to get there. It becomes less about the labor and ingenuity and more about the goal itself—the end becomes too important, and the means to the end less so. And when ambitious people are more focused on getting what they want and less on getting it the right way, problems start to arise.

For a real-life example of how this works, look at lobbyist Jack Abramoff. Before being convicted of conspiracy and mail fraud in 2006, he was a huge power broker with a promising career in Washington, D.C.

Abramoff showed ambition at an early age, attending Brandeis University and Georgetown University law school. After graduating from Brandeis, Abramoff successfully ran for the national chairmanship of the College Republicans. According to an article in *Mother Jones*, Abramoff "purged" the organization of moderates in its leadership ranks in favor of "hard core" conservative ideologues. Abramoff would become a staunch Reagan Republican and, in fact, mobilized a large student turnout in Massachusetts during the 1980 presidential elections. A former teacher of Abramoff's describes his core beliefs as being "so strong . . . he was like steel."

Abramoff continued his enthusiasm as a lobbyist for conservative causes in D.C. Ironically, as *Mother Jones* points out, at one time, Abramoff considered lobbyists "evil" and he took his first lobbying job under the condition that he would be able to "advocate only for the positions that he believed in." Many considered his idealism and work ethic admirable. Unfortunately, Abramoff allowed his ambition to turn him from a purist into someone who illegally and unethically misused his political muscle.

In his burning desire for authority and access, Abramoff offered jobs, restaurant meals, golf trips to Scotland, tickets to Washington Redskins games, and more to congressional staffers and White House officials. He tried to get people in his pocket hired into positions of influence, and even orchestrated lobbying against his own clients behind their backs to force them to pay for more of his lobbying services to counter . . . his own influence. When the news of his corruption started to break, his colleague Kevin Ring (who himself was later convicted of conspiracy to corrupt public officials) said, "This could be the Enron of lobbying." And indeed it was.

Some people who get away with illegal or unethical methods for achieving great success see a certain glamour in the way in which they operate outside of the rules. They start to believe that laws apply to everyone else, not them. It puts them in a separate, special class of achiever, which lets them further justify their bad behavior. "What I do is acceptable, even desirable, in the world in which I operate, and the proof of that is the fact that I've benefited from it," is the thinking. This is a very dangerous, insulated place from which to operate, because the overly ambitious person comes to believe he is truly living in an alternate reality, much like the mafia.

In fact, according to reports, Abramoff liked to perform Michael Corleone's dialogue from *The Godfather*. He'd mimic Michael Corleone, eyes narrowed, going head-to-head with politicians who demanded a cut of the Corleone family's earnings: "Senator, you can have my answer now if you like. My offer is this: nothing." What kind of politico quotes Michael Corleone? Why revel in a line of dialogue uttered by a criminal, a fictional one, no less? Abramoff was drunk on his own ambition, without empathy for his own clients, with an utter lack of perspective.

In the end, Abramoff pleaded guilty to felony counts involving fraud, corruption, and conspiracy. He was sentenced to four years in prison. He served three and a half years at a minimum-security prison and was released in 2010. Upon his release, still under the supervision of the Bureau of Prisons, Abramoff worked as an accountant at a Baltimore Pizza shop for the remaining six months of his four-year sentence while living at a halfway house until his final release in December 2010.

I think his fall illustrates both corporate and personal ambition run amok. This man's place in the world, the world's perspective of him, with his sharp hats and suits, was vital to him. His ambition to make a name for himself, to be the go-to guy, caused him to instead become a convicted felon.

Explosive Ambition Formula 2: Ambition Plus Impatience

The temptation to take shortcuts is something many people with an otherwise admirable ambition fall prey to. When you want something so badly, and you've been working for a long time to achieve your goal, it can be very tempting to circumvent obstacles and just get there already. Remember that ambition is the fuel that propels you on a journey to success. This journey is long and often full of roadblocks, detours, and other obstacles. Truly ambitious people who use their gifts correctly don't get sidetracked by these temporary impediments on the path to their ultimate destination. They build in the time and the expectation for setbacks. In other words, when ambition is in balance it allows for both success and failure. People with healthy ambition learn from their failures in order to refine their skills and critical thinking abilities.

Unfortunately, while ambition provides the initial drive, it can sometimes fail to equip people for a journey that is more than likely going to be a frustrating uphill battle. Achieving your goals is always going to be hard work. But if you're not willing to do what it takes, it's much better to change your goals (or temper them to be more achievable in the short term) than to start cutting corners.

Professional athletes are in a particularly tough spot when it comes to resisting the temptation to take shortcuts. They have a short time frame in which they operate at their peak physical performance; no matter how good they are today, they are constantly aware that if they don't push themselves to the extreme, then they will quickly be replaced tomorrow.

The fact that the careers of professional athletes often peak when they are in their twenties underscores the pressures they face to rise above the pack and stay in the spotlight for as long as possible—by any means possible. The ultra-ambitious Marion Jones is a sad story of someone who took a shortcut toward meeting her ambition, and paid the price for it.

Jones was an Olympic runner whose epic abilities were called into question and ultimately discredited after she became a target in the BALCO doping scandal in 2007.

Jones's story goes back to her youth, when her stepdad, a stay-at-home father with whom she was extraordinarily close, suddenly died. Jones was a very young girl. She took up running to cope with her grief. Almost instantly she became very good at it. At fourteen, she won the first of four California sprint titles. At fifteen, she was competing in the U.S. national championships. It seemed that Jones was on track to achieve her ambitious goals: as early as the age of eight, inspired by the 1984 Olympic games, Jones wrote on her chalkboard, "I will be an Olympic champion."

In college she met and began dating track coach and Olympic hopeful C. J. Hunter—the two soon married. They trained together for the 2000 Olympics. The couple shared a coach, and this coach became known for his dealings with BALCO, a lab that provided steroids to a number of athletes. Eventually it was announced that Jones's husband C.J. had failed numerous drug tests. Jones sat grimly by his side as he was booted from the Olympics.

Jones, however, trained hard and made a lot of sacrifices. Her coach said, "Marion literally never has missed a day of practice . . . and she is never late." Her "secret," wrote John Hendershott of *Track & Field News* in the late 1990s, is that "beneath her radiant smile and outgoing manner is a relentless drive to succeed, a white-hot intensity to learn just how good she can become." Many placed high hopes on her potential for the upcoming 2000 Olympic games. In an *LA Times* article, Craig Masback, the CEO of USA Track and Field, said Jones had "the chance to be the first female international athlete to transcend sports. In my mind, only three people have done that: Pele, Muhammad Ali and Michael Jordan."

It looked like Jones was on track. She went on to win three gold medals and two bronzes in 2000. It was a truly amazing haul. But the whispers about Jones's own steroid use, which had, in fact, begun years earlier, got louder. In 2007, just eight months after she got married to her second husband, the evidence of Jones's drug use became too obvious to ignore. According to *The Washington Post*, citing unidentified sources with knowledge of drug results from the USA track and field championships in Indianapolis, on "June 23, 2006, an 'A' sample of Marion Jones's urine tested positive for Erythropoietin (EPO), a banned performance-enhancer." Jones's world came crashing down, and she admitted to taking steroids before the 2000 Olympics. She made a public apology and was stripped of her medals, finally serving a sentence of six months in a federal prison.

It is heartbreaking to consider all of the real training that she did, the real time she spent practicing, the real pains she suffered and sacrifices she made—all for nothing. Who knows what would have happened if Jones hadn't had a performance enhancer in her system? Obviously there's no way to know, but she must not have believed herself capable of meeting her ambition without cutting corners. Jones inhabited a world where doping was, if not the norm, something people around her did, and the temptation was too great. But the consequences of the illegal substances were clear. Shortly after she admitted taking banned substances, the president of the International Association of Athletics Federations said, "Marion Jones will be remembered as one of the biggest frauds in sporting history."

Explosive Ambition Formula 3: Ambition Plus Greed

Greed and ambition do not necessarily go hand in hand. One could have an ambition, like Kathleen the nurse, to help others, or one like Bill Gates, that results in financial rewards but is not primarily motivated by the desire for such rewards. But because money is often equated with success in our culture (and of course because of all the desirable things money can buy), greed is often wrapped up in ambition. Ironically, ambition that is used to feed pure unadulterated greed often requires just as much work and intelligence as healthy ambition.

Let's look at Ken Lay and Jeff Skilling, the guys who took down Enron by cooking their company's books and lying about it. In January 2000, Enron's actual earnings per share were .30, but the company claimed they were .31, in line with what Wall Street had anticipated they'd be. In July 2000, when Wall Street's anticipation was that Enron's earnings would be at .32 a share, the company claimed they were at .34 a share. Enron was outperforming everyone's expectations; no wonder the company was named *Fortune* magazine's Most Innovative Company in America in February 2001, as well as one of the top twenty most admired companies and one of the top twenty in quality of management. With investor confidence in Enron management flying high, stock prices rose as high as $90 a share.

But as we know now, the company's success was built on a foundation of greed-fueled lies. "The company had long-running, very deep and difficult" economic issues, said Ben Glisan Jr., a former employee and CPA of the company. Glisan went on to admit that he lied about the health of the company, inflated its earning reports, and hid its debt, all while handing out big bonuses to the executives.

Eventually, that foundation crumbled, taking down the entire company, which filed for bankruptcy in December 2001, and also thousands of employees whose lives and savings were drastically changed for the worse. What caused this? Pure ambition and greed. Enron's executives let a future-time perspective give way to a present-time perspective, choosing to value immediate returns over long-term growth and health. As Philip Zimbardo and John Boyd wrote in *The Time Paradox,* Enron had a culture that valued instant gratification; its present-oriented leaders could justify falsifying earnings reports because they didn't look far enough ahead into the future to imagine the consequences if they were ever caught. They only looked toward the next earnings statement, three months away.

You can't run a successful business without looking more

than three months into the future. But in the heat of the Wall Street moment, it's easy to lose perspective. Andrew Lo, a professor at the Massachusetts Institute of Technology's Sloan School of Management, published research showing that when stock traders have a good day in the market, the flood of dopamine in their brains creates a surge of overconfidence. "They believe they've achieved this good fortune themselves," writes David Brooks in *The Social Animal: The Hidden Sources of Love, Character, and Achievement.* "They have figured out the market. They become blind to downside risk."

Not everyone is equally susceptible to greed, even in a climate where short-term gains are valued. In fact, Enron's VP of corporate development and the whistle-blower of this crisis, Sherron Watkins, tried to voice the minority opinion, but was a victim of the kind of groupthink denial discussed in chapter 2. In her book *Power Failure: The Inside Story of the Collapse of Enron,* Watkins says that she wrote to CEO Ken Lay in August 2001: "I am incredibly nervous that we will implode in a wave of accounting scandals. My eight years of Enron work history will be worth nothing on my resume, the business world will consider the past successes nothing but an elaborate accounting hoax." Her mind unclouded by greed, Watkins was able to see the big picture. As Zimbardo put it:

How could a group of smart people be so dumb? Well, they weren't dumb. The complex—and fraudulent—financial transactions that they used to inflate Enron earnings were extremely sophisticated and inventive.

They were very clever, and initially, most likely future-oriented, or they never would have gotten as far as they did in business. Over time, though, greed dissolved their future orientation and replaced it with a present orientation that excluded the prospect of getting caught as a dirty rotten scoundrel. In the end, they saw no further than the next earnings report. Unlike Lay, Skilling and the rest, Watkins saw the connection between the past, present and future. She wanted her past success to have a positive effect on her personal future, not to destroy it.

Watkins will be remembered in a positive way, as the whistle-blower who spoke truth to power. But the name Enron now symbolizes the worst kind of corporate evil and excess. And of course it was a precursor to a much larger financial meltdown in 2008, another one caused by out-of-control ambition and greed, unrestrained by ethics or a long-term future-time-oriented perspective.

Explosive Ambition Formula 4: Ambition Plus Narcissism

Narcissism is an expressed thought or behavior that places the self above all others, no matter the cost. The American Psychological Association describes narcissistic personality disorder (NPD) as a "pervasive pattern of grandiosity, need for admiration, and a lack of empathy." Narcissism is related to the ego issues that we talked about in the first chapter, but is different in that the focus on the self is blinding in a way that mere ego is not. I believe that many ambitious people who find themselves in crises tend to display more narcissistic tendencies than the average person. That's not to say that narcissism makes a person ambitious or that ambition causes narcissism. I only mean that when an ambitious person is in a mess, quite often narcissism played a big role.

Politicians, especially those in the national spotlight, are often jokingly accused of being narcissists but, in all seriousness, their profession lends itself to this particularly destructive personality trait. For example, in order to be a successful candidate, you have to be unnaturally optimistic even in the face of probable defeat and possess high levels of self-esteem despite the constant criticism that comes with the territory. Furthermore, you are constantly given sole credit for successes—even though those successes were achieved, in part, by the work of many aides and assistants. Finally, you constantly have people relying on you, believing in you, and holding you responsible as the sole representative of a cause. All of this power can lead to an exaggerated sense of self-importance that can cause some individuals to believe that the world revolves around them. That's when their out-of-control behaviors become easier to rationalize.

Consider, for example, John Edwards. He had a great story. He was born into poverty, with his dad working in the local textile mill and his mom working as a mail carrier. He was the first person in his family to go to college. His first date with the woman who became his wife was at Wendy's. Elizabeth Edwards was a sympathetic, popular potential First

Lady, one who had struggled with cancer and was admired for her courage. In 2008, things looked good for Edwards on the political front. His ambitions—to be president—looked as though they had a good shot of being realized.

Except somewhere along the line, Edwards's narcissistic tendencies started making news. Narcissists are led by warped moral compasses. Because narcissists are the center of their own universe, they do not consider how their actions negatively affect others. They cannot empathize with the pain others are experiencing, pain often inflicted by the narcissists themselves. During his campaign, when Elizabeth's cancer recurred and was deemed terminal, Edwards was outed as having an affair with Rielle Hunter, a videographer on his campaign. Making matters worse, Hunter was pregnant, and Edwards's campaign aide Andrew Young initially claimed that he was the father of Hunter's baby. It smacked of ridiculousness and desperation, with Young seemingly throwing himself on his sword for his boss. When Young fessed up, he made Edwards look even more venal and ridiculous. In his autobiography, Young wrote that Edwards had promised Hunter that he'd marry her as soon as his wife died, and the Dave Matthews Band would play at their wedding. Young said that Edwards told him to steal one of the baby's used diapers so that Edwards could perform his own DNA test to be sure the baby really was his. Clearly, Edwards's narcissism got in the way of his otherwise admirable ambitions.

In 2011 a federal grand jury indicted Edwards on six felony charges including conspiracy, accepting illegal campaign funds, and making false statements. Prosecutors say he used nearly $1 million in campaign funds to pay for expenses related to the upkeep, prenatal care, and hiding of Hunter. Edwards contends that the funds were never campaign contributions, but were personal donations to help a friend in a fix. He pleaded not guilty to six counts of violating federal campaign laws. After his indictment, Edwards told reporters: "I will regret for the rest of my life the pain and the harm that I've caused to others. . . . But I did not break the law. And I never, ever thought that I was breaking the law." If found guilty he could face thirty years in prison and $1.5 million in fines.

There have been many theories offered up to explain how Edwards could be so careless—truly baffling considering he had so much to lose and did it in a way that was so obnoxious and crude. Why was being a contender for president and having a loving family, as it appeared he did from the outside, not enough for him? Why did his ambitions and narcissism allow him to believe he could have it all—the presidency, a mistress, and allegedly illegal misuse of funds from his campaigns—all things that would threaten what he built and seemed to care for?

Edwards is an almost Shakespearean example of how ambition combined with narcissism can cost you not only the thing you're trying to get but also everything you currently have. I'm not trying to excuse Edwards's behavior with the above theories, merely to explore how certain aspects of his personality may have contributed to his downfall. We often don't want to examine the darker sides of our personality because we think we would never be "that person," but ambition can be all-consuming and feed on itself—the more you have, the more you want. If this tendency is left unchecked, it's easy to lose focus and have your ambition fueled by other negative qualities. It is one of those traits that can easily attach itself to other unbalanced aspects of our bad self. In Edwards's case, fear and denial also played a big role in derailing his ambition.

Let's use the POWER model to look at where John Edwards failed to control his ambition and how he could have rectified the situation.

Edwards correctly pinpointed and recognized his ambitious behavior—he knew that he wanted to run for office and that he would do anything it would take to get there. It is unclear whether he weighed where Rielle Hunter fit into those ambitions. I suspect not, that the decision was not conscious, just a vague sense that what he had was no longer enough. For most people, and especially ambitious people, "as soon as they accomplish something they want to accomplish the next best thing," psychologist John Gartner told ABC news. "There is a tendency to move the goalposts and to expand the sphere of their ambition to a point where it's overly grandiose." This fits with research on motivation and happiness. Psychologists Phillip Brickman and Donald Campbell theorized that once we experience a major positive event in our life, we habituate to the level of happiness that it brings. Later, these same experiences no longer provide the same satisfaction. To get the same high and sustain a feeling of achievement, we must seek out a more intense experience to satisfy ourselves. Perhaps that's where Hunter fit in—the happiness and excitement she brought Edwards fed his heightened need.

Unfortunately Edwards did not own the negative consequences of his behavior with Hunter until it was too late—
whether he was in denial or not, Edwards didn't weigh the
potential consequences of his actions thoroughly enough to
avoid having the affair that could jeopardize everything.

He does seem to have worked things through. In a 2008
interview given to ABC News's Bob Woodruff, Edwards said
that his situation "fed a self-focus egotism, a narcissism that
leads you to believe that you can do whatever you want." The
first step is admitting you have a problem—only time will tell
if Edwards will continue such introspection in an effort to
change for the better. If Edwards had owned his ambition and
really internalized how much scrutiny he would be under as a
candidate, he might not have had the affair; on the flip side, if
he had already been unfaithful to his wife and really accepted
responsibility for that, he might not have run for office and
thus might have avoided the word getting out about his actions in such a painful and humiliating way.

Edwards failed to *explore* how his actions could affect his
marriage, his family, his image, and his chances for a successful
presidential candidacy. He did not wrap his head around the
high standards that presidents—and candidates—are held to,
and he did not learn from the examples of so many other politicians whose careers had been leveled by scandals before him.
Edwards needed to separate his ambition from his narcissism
and sexual proclivities. He needed to accept that his sexual
proclivities would damage his ability to achieve his goals; he
should have reined them in and kept himself focused on his
long-term dreams rather than his short-term whims.

Explosive Ambition Formula 5: Ambition Plus Loss of Focus

What all of the examples above have in common is that another element—ego, hedonism, greed—influences ambitious people and they lose focus on what they really want. These other elements cause the ambitious person to take his eyes off the prize (or in the case of John Edwards, decide that the prize wasn't big enough). In many ways, this is why it is imperative to constantly check your motivations so that you are proceeding toward the right goal for the right reasons. It's so easy to lose focus on what you are actually trying to achieve.

A clear example of unfocused ambition leading to disaster can be found in the Duke lacrosse case. In this example, the prosecutor, Mike Nifong, got caught up in the media frenzy that surrounded the case. I believe his ambition to pursue justice was trumped by the desire to make a name for himself. He channeled the same ambition that got him to this position of power into snatching the glory and fame that would be associated with a successful prosecution in such a high-profile case. Misguided ambition torpedoed his career. If you've forgotten, the story went something like this:

In 2006, the Duke men's lacrosse team was having a party at an off-campus house and ordered up a stripper. After the party, the exotic dancer in question, Crystal Gail Mangum, accused some of the young men of rape. The Durham, North Carolina, prosecutor of the case, Nifong, leveled rape and other charges against three of the Duke students. There was a huge rush to judgment against the athletes. The story was nearly irresistible gossip fodder, with its poor black stripper, entitled white meathead athletes, and avenging prosecutor, an obvious narrative about town tensions and race relations in the South. But just because it's a good story doesn't make it true. This case may well have been the career-maker Nifong was hoping for, but his ambition shifted from, one assumes, wanting to do a bang-up job and attain justice, to leveraging the case to enhance his career.

Nifong gave over fifty interviews with the national media—that's a lot of publicity courting. He made attention-getting but prejudicial public statements, such as calling the lacrosse players hooligans whose "daddies could buy them expensive lawyers." If his true ambition was to have an admirable career, what Nifong should have done was pay attention to the evidence, and the fact that the alleged victim had serious credibility issues. Compelling evidence of the boys' guilt simply wasn't there . . . which was probably why Nifong wound up suppressing evidence that would have exculpated them.

When it became clear that Nifong had withheld DNA evidence that could have helped clear the boys' names, the state bar association filed ethics charges against him for withholding evidence, making inflammatory public statements about the case, and showing a "systematic abuse of prosecutorial discretion." The attorney general pointed out, "There were many points in this case where caution would have served justice better than bravado." Indeed. But bravado gets publicity and caution doesn't. Nifong was ultimately disbarred.

Nifong probably thought that the end justified the means, at least at first. He may have even thought the lacrosse players were, in fact, guilty. He would do whatever was necessary to put them away. But he was so eager to get to the finish line and secure a conviction in the hopes of reaping the rewards and acclaim that would surely follow, that he wound up making critical mistakes. Instead of suppressing evidence, he should have taken the opportunity to reevaluate the narrative.

Applying the POWER Model

Pinpoint the core trait: In this case, ambition.
Own it: Acknowledge that it can be both good and bad.
Work it through: Process the role it's played in your life.
Explore it: Consider how it could play out in the future.
Rein it in: Establish how to reachieve balance and control.

PINPOINT that you are ambitious.

OWN IT: When you own your ambition, you recognize that it has a positive and a negative side, and you consider personal morality in what you do as you strive for personal accomplishment. Without ambition we would have no forward momentum, but with too much ambition, we risk losing friends, family, life balance, and our ethical compass. Ambition can give our lives meaning, provide for our families, make us feel jazzed and competitive (in a good way) and fulfilled . . . but it can also cause us to behave in boorish and unethical ways or can make us sacrifice everything we've strived for. Your goal in this is to balance both so that you move forward with your life while avoiding crisis.

WORK IT THROUGH: If you work through your feelings about ambition, you'll probably find you have mixed feelings about it. Consider the messages you've received about ambition from your family and your community: Is any amount of ambition seen as making someone a "self-promoter" and regarded as unseemly? Are you supposed to be modest to a fault, not admitting that you're really hungry for leadership roles and recognition? Or, on the flip side, are you supposed to strive to reach the top at any cost? Does your family define "ambition" narrowly (marriage and children, for example) while you, given your druthers, would choose to define it in another way (a career and the opportunity to travel, say)? Is taking time to smell the roses something you or your family have always viewed as a sign of laziness or a lack of direction?

EXPLORE IT: Explore these ideas by considering what would happen if you allowed ambition to have balance in your life—what if you found some kind of parity between work and personal life? Consider whether you're afraid of failure or whether you've cut corners and burned bridges to get what you want.

REIN IT IN: And finally, if you see that you don't like the person you're becoming because of your all-consuming ambition, or conversely if you don't like the person you're becoming because you've been too fearful about actually striving for something you want, take action to rein it in. If your issue has been allowing ambition to run roughshod over you, what might it be like to dial it back? Would you be less happy if you spent more time with your family or decided that your conscience should from here on out dictate how your ambition plays out? Rein in the attitudes toward ambition that have been damaging to you and—with honesty and self-respect—take the steps you have to take to get on the right road.

5.

ACCOMMODATION

FINDING
THE MIDDLE GROUND

I so wanted to ask this basketball superstar for an autograph for my son, but it wouldn't be professional. I was meeting with him, his lawyer, and his agent. Their client had been pulled over by the police for a traffic violation while driving his brand-new Bentley. In the course of the stop, the police noticed a sizable bag of marijuana in the backseat of the car. He swore it wasn't his and that it must have been left by one of his friends who frequently borrowed the car. He assured us that these friends weren't drug dealers, though; they just liked to get high . . . a lot.

"And you still lent them the car?" I asked.

He told me that they were his "boys" and that they all grew up together—it wouldn't be right not to share his success with them. He wanted them to know that despite his fame, he was still the same old guy from back in the day. I had to tell him that he might be the same guy, but he was in a totally different situation now. I reminded him that he was a high-profile athlete with a great deal of endorsements and that it might benefit him to remember that before making such decisions. For his own good, he had to draw boundaries. Sometimes he had to say no.

———

Flick on the TV and channel surf for a few minutes. The words you're likely to hear as you pass through the news and commercials are along the lines of, "stand up to stains!" "candidate faces pushback," "fight fat," and any number of combative words that typify the in-your-face climate we seem to live in. In this era of assertiveness training, the notion of being accommodating is often sneered at and dismissed as weakness. That's just silly. The ability to accommodate can be a huge strength. From the first day of nursery school, children absorb the rules of sharing and respect in a classroom—that's accommodation. Kids are being taught how to coexist in a civilized society, because that's what they will need to do for the rest of their lives.

A "make my day" attitude might be flashier, but being accommodating to your fellow human beings is one of the most essential skills in life. It means making room for others in your space, which sometimes involves forgoing your own immediate comfort and sacrificing for the good of the society, the family, or the company. It's what makes a workplace tick. It's what makes family reunions tolerable. It's what makes you a good friend, an effective boss, and the kind of parent whose children feel loved and nurtured. Accommodation is the social glue that holds us together. People who understand the need to assist and sometimes yield to others are more likely to have allies and a more complete understanding of the environment. These are two critical assets to have that can help prevent and mitigate crisis.

Still, accommodation also exists along a spectrum. At one end we have "too accommodating," while at the other we have "non-accommodating." The too-accommodating personality is defined as one that constantly puts others before itself to the point that it becomes detrimental, not just to the individual but sometimes to the greater system. Others learn that they don't have to take your needs into consideration because you'll never stand up for yourself. You end up being seen as a pushover and risk becoming irrelevant or taken for granted. This is a whole life problem, because unlike some traits, say denial and fear, that are often compartmentalized to certain situations and contexts, accommodation is a trait that seems to spill over into many aspects of life—if someone is a pushover in the workplace, he or she is more than likely a pushover in relationships and everyday interactions. I believe that when people are overly accommodating, they give up their own self-worth to gain the approval of others.

On the other far end of the spectrum, the person who is non-accommodating is pigheaded, uncooperative, and even hostile. Those who fail to accommodate others are generally seen as selfish; they rely heavily on ego to justify their lack of flexibility and are not team players. Being perceived as selfish, inflexible, and non-accommodating can leave you dangerously isolated and without allies.

As with all of the attributes in this book, a balanced level of accommodation is what you're striving for, by modulating how accommodating you are so that it's appropriate to the situation you're in, and being sure you're comfortable with any long-term consequences of it. This chapter looks at the character trait and situational contexts of accommodation. We'll look at how accommodation can be advantageous or harmful depending on the circumstances, and we'll talk about how to use the POWER model to get your level of accommodation where it will work optimally for you.

Accommodation in All Areas of Life

Any time you have two people or groups with conflicting goals or needs, a certain amount of accommodation by both sides is necessary to resolve the issue. In conflict situations, such as in the political arena, collaboration on a compromise in which each side accommodates the other is often the strategy that produces a win-win scenario; neither side has to give up more than it can stomach because with a little give and take, both sides find a way to solve the problem that everyone can accept.

Unfortunately, especially in the political arena, things have become so polarized that no one wants to appear weak by accommodating. That's a huge mistake, as evidenced by what took place in 2011. That summer, Americans and the world witnessed one of the most cantankerous debates in modern political history. What made it so surprising was that it was over a rather common procedural process (raising the debt ceiling) that had occurred many times in the past under both Democratic and Republican presidents. Any person or group is much more likely to be accommodating if the other person or group is likewise in a conciliatory mood. But because "accommodation" has become a dirty word, both sides bitterly fought to defend their party's position.

In brief, both sides knew that unless the debt ceiling was raised, America would default on money it had borrowed, which "would have catastrophic economic consequences that would last for decades," according to Tim Geithner, the U.S. Treasury Secretary. It would, he said, spur ruinously high interest rates and threaten the dollar's dominant role in the international financial system. Both sides agreed that spending cuts were necessary to keep future debt down, but disagreed on how much and which cuts should be made. Republicans essentially refused to raise the debt ceiling to pay for already incurred debts, in order to lock in their agenda for the future; Democrats felt that they were being held hostage, and didn't want to make big cuts to programs such as Social Security, but rather wanted to raise taxes to decrease the deficit. This difference of opinion aside, they had a more immediate job to do: pass the basic procedural bill that would ensure that the government could pay the bills for debts already incurred.

The president, trying to get the two sides to accommodate one another, cited the fact that the debt ceiling had been routinely raised in the past—eighteen times under Ronald Reagan, nine times under George H. W. Bush, six times under Bill Clinton, and seven times under George W. Bush. But to the Tea Party freshmen, President Obama was missing the point. The fact that it had become routine was exactly the problem. They saw their jobs as elected representatives as not to proceed with business as usual, but to implement real change. The parties battled it out—in Congress, in the White House, and all over the media—for weeks.

Television pundits on both sides argued which side was being obstructionist, but the overall effect of the infantile squabbling and lack of accommodation was a sense of instability and concrete financial ramifications. Standard & Poors, a financial credit ratings agency, downgraded the U.S.'s treasury rating, an indication of its opinion that the country was not as good a credit risk as it had been when the government played nicer. Many experts believed that such a downgrade would have a significant impact on treasury rates over time. Terry Belton, global head of fixed-income strategy at JPMorgan, suggested that the downgrade could cost taxpayers $100 billion. "That $100 billion a year is money being used for higher interest rates and that's money being taken away from other goods and services." Politico suggested that the debt ceiling debacle "crushed American confidence like few recent events and may well help tip the economy back toward recession." Public faith in the government to solve financial problems dropped, and various polls reported both Republican and Democratic voters were overwhelmingly frustrated, and not just with the outcome of the debt ceiling debates; they felt a "disgust" with the "ridiculous" way their elected officials acted. The whole debacle highlights a situation where accommodation can be a beneficial strategy if it helps to achieve a larger goal, and disastrous if you are unable to reach an accommodation.

The lesson to be learned here is that oftentimes in a conflict, resolving the conflict is more important than the individual aims of either side. When you find yourself in situations where it seems as though the other side is refusing to cooperate, if you want to move forward, you need to look at the situation through their eyes first. Whether you agree with the rationale or not, you have to accept—or at least acknowledge—the other side's position if you ever want to begin to solve the problem. Both sides in this case were aware of the other's position, but neither was willing to cede enough to move on.

Sometimes you will find that both sides have the same goal, but disagree about the correct path. Here, I do believe they shared a secondary goal—cutting spending—but had different primary goals, and those were partisan. Both of their primary goals should have been to resolve the debt ceiling issue and to protect the stability of the markets. In the end, a resolution was forced, no one was happy with the outcome anyway, and real damage was done to the U.S.'s economic standing.

Accommodating Friends and Family
When working with opponents in politics, sometimes you have to lose the battle if you want to win the war. At times, being willing to give up on certain concessions in order to prevent a crisis does not mean you are weak; it means you are smart. That is true in most relationships in life as well. But in many marriages, as in politics, thoughtful consideration is seldom given to opposing viewpoints and oftentimes there is little respect between the parties involved.

Everyone knows intellectually that a marriage requires

give-and-take. But every couple that I've encountered in a crisis situation has trouble putting that basic truth into practice. Sometimes, you have to accommodate a spouse's needs. One person, for example, will work while the other furthers his or her education for the good of the marriage and the family. Maybe you will have to deal with a spouse's mood swings and inattentiveness while he or she is going through a difficult time, with the expectation that that person would put up with your unpleasant quirks when you are going through a bad patch. In almost all marriages, a healthy amount of accommodation is necessary in order for the marriage to survive. The ideal is that the two people involved don't feel that their spouse is asking for more than he or she gives back at some point, or doesn't experience accommodating the other as a huge burden.

When this balance between partners is in place, things work. It doesn't always mean accommodation is easy, but it goes along with commitment. But what happens when it's only one person who is giving while the other is constantly taking? It happens in more couples than you would think and you can't always tell from the outside that it's going on. While it's easy to simply place the blame on the person who takes advantage of someone's passivity, the more passive partner is just as responsible in a different way, in that he may be too accommodating and needs to fight for what he wants and needs.

I have a friend who is a throwback to the old days of traditional male/female gender roles. He met his wife while he was finishing up a prestigious MBA program and she was getting her degree in education. He was instantly attracted to her intelligence, beauty, humor, and warmth, and after a brief courtship, they married and began their lives together. In the beginning, they both worked—she with special-needs children. Special education was her passion and working with children in this capacity was what she always wanted to do. He accepted a position with a company and would soon be on the fast track to the management ranks.

The first signs of trouble in their marriage came with the mixed blessing of his wife's first pregnancy. They were thrilled at the prospect of starting a family, but he pushed her to quit her job and be a stay-at-home mom—just for a few years, he promised. She reluctantly agreed but when she got pregnant with her second child, the timeline for her return to work was pushed back yet again.

Throughout those years, my friend thought they had the perfect marriage—he would often surprise his wife with jewelry or vacations and would even send her flowers for no reason at all. I really believe he loved her dearly.

But she began to grow frustrated and tired of constantly giving in to his idea of who she should be. She loved him and her kids, but she wanted more. Several times they discussed her returning to work, and several times, "it was decided" that it was better for her primary job to be that of a full-time mom. I put that phrase in quotes because he decided and she ultimately agreed, but it wasn't an equal conversation in which she felt heard. She may have agreed, but not happily so, and that was bound to backfire.

Then something completely unexpected happened. My friend's company downsized and he lost his job. After months of searching for employment, he found another, but it paid considerably less than his previous one. So in order to make ends meet, his wife took a job at a local elementary school. Because she had been out of work for so long, though, she was only able to secure a part-time teacher's-assistant position. But despite the less-than-ideal circumstances, his wife loved her newfound sense of purpose. She began to make new friends, discover new interests, and redevelop the sense of identity that she had lost over the years. She even toyed with the idea of returning to graduate school.

That's when my friend began complaining to me. He was resentful when his wife would take extra time to help a student at the school or when he had to cook dinner for himself. Even though they were both working, he expected things to be the same as they always had been. And in some ways, you can see why he would. He was used to her accommodating him. His wife had supported him all those years—going to his work functions, putting up with his moods during stressful periods of work, and postponing her dreams of teaching so that he could pursue his career and their kids would have a full-time parent. He appreciated it, but he was not willing to do the same for her and was utterly confused when she began to, in his words, "change." I tried to gently point out to him that he needed to support his wife and be more accommodating to her needs, because she had done the same for him for so many years.

Several years later, after both kids were in college, my friend returned home to find his wife gone and her belongings packed up. She had had enough. Apparently she no longer felt obligated to stay in a marriage where she had accommodated the needs of her husband while he refused to support her in her endeavors. While I was shocked at the abruptness of her decision (at least from where I sat—for all I know she gave him plenty of warnings), I can't say I was exactly surprised. The marriage did not have a healthy give-and-take—it was give give give on her part and take take take on his.

There were other factors besides how unaccommodating he was (and how overly so she was) that led to the dramatic end of my friend's marriage. For example, he was in denial about his wife's unhappiness, and his failure to balance work and home life probably also contributed to the problem. His ego, too, probably contributed to his belief that his wife would never leave him. In fact, she always went along with what he asked of her—but that right there was part of the problem. While we might always hope that the person we are married to has enough sense to "read between the lines," the truth is that if we constantly attend to their needs without standing up for our own, they don't always realize how unhappy we are. She may have spoken up about her needs more than I knew, but didn't insist that they be met. I don't know why—perhaps she was afraid to change the status quo, or didn't think dealing with his anger was worth it. And he didn't step up. In the end, his failure to accommodate her needs and her tendency to over-accommodate his led to the failure of their marriage.

Accommodation and Our Children

In many cases, in our efforts to give our kids the best of everything, we are doing them more harm than good. It might seem as though we are helping them by making sure they have every possible resource and advantage—accommodating them. But in fact we are handicapping their ability to learn to take care of themselves. There is a wealth of research on this subject; child development experts from Dan Kindlon (author of *Too Much of a Good Thing: Raising Children of Character in an Indulgent Age*) to Madeline Levine (*The Price of Privilege: How Parental Pressure and Material Advantage Are Creating a Generation of Disconnected and Unhappy Kids*) to Wendy Mogel (*The Blessing of a Skinned Knee: Using Jewish Teachings to Raise Self-Reliant Children*) have all written thoughtfully on the risks to and unhappiness of today's generation of pampered young people.

They have found that overly indulged children who never learn to fail, who never come to understand that they can survive without parental hovering, who never have to do chores, who never flunk a math test because of persistent parental tutoring or intervention with teachers—are kids who are more likely to wind up weakened, incapacitated, unable to deal with a world that is not as generous as their parents.

It doesn't end when the kids grow up, either. Imagine the situation of a mother with an adult child who comes to her for money every month after she continually mismanages her spending. The mom finally refuses to accommodate and enable her daughter; she declares that she will no longer pay her daughter's rent when she herself is working hard to make ends meet. After this declaration, the relationship might be strained. The daughter will most likely accuse her mother of not loving her—logical, since that's how the mother showed love up until that moment—and may even refuse to talk to her again. However, in the long run, it's healthier for the mother not to accommodate her daughter. It's also healthier (although harder) for the daughter to not be accommodated so she can (hopefully) learn to manage her funds better.

Many over-accommodated children are so used to being catered to that they haven't learned how to care for the needs of others. They're not as well equipped to handle disappointment, delayed gratification, or conflict. Instead of valuing hard work, they feel entitled to everything that's been handed to them. These kids become massively non-accommodating because the nursery school skills of sharing, waiting, and compromising were never reinforced at home.

The MTV show *My Super Sweet 16* is the problem writ large. One of the worst reality shows in recent memory, it's a docudrama that follows a young girl or boy who is turning sixteen. Often, their families are portrayed as being very wealthy and well connected. The parents, in an effort to either please their children or validate their own standing in the community (remember, over-accommodating people often lack internal validation and seek outside sources to confirm their self-worth), throw their obnoxious teenagers the most extravagant parties that money can buy, complete with ponies and appearances by pop idols and price tags on par with a wedding for 200. The children are usually shown as bratty, unruly, and ungrateful.

I'm sure they come off worse because of the editing, but still, I've seen this type of behavior over and over again with parents and their children. Parents are afraid that their love won't be understood unless they translate it into a material thing—a car, new clothes, etc. They let poor behavior slide and rationalize it away because they don't want their kids to dislike them. They want to make their kids happy and don't realize that they're making them unappreciative and unprepared for the real world.

Accommodation in the Workplace

Sarah, a middle manager at a small manufacturing company, was a classic accommodator. She was the person her coworkers called on to take care of last-minute projects for them. She never failed to "pitch in" on things that had little to do with her job description; she perpetually found herself working late or taking work home over the weekend. She prided herself on being indispensable, but what she called "indispensable" looked to me like "unappreciated." Her self-image was that of the "get-along girl"—someone who is always easy to work with, never makes waves, forever carries a heavy load without complaint.

Sarah thought this would pay off in the form of a raise and a promotion, but her boss knew a good thing when he had it; even though she was at an associate's level within the organization, he kept asking her to pick up his dry cleaning or grab a birthday present for his kid if his own assistant (who was far better at setting boundaries than Sarah was) was unavailable.

Her boss liked her right where she was—at his beck and call. Instead, he promoted members of the team he perceived as more aggressive and less reactive. Sarah fantasized about quitting, imagining the way everyone would suddenly realize with sorrow and regret just how vital she was to the organization. But she never gave voice to her feelings of being undervalued.

You can see the problem. People who overly accommodate at work rarely get the opportunity to stand out. They risk becoming the workplace pushover, the go-to grunt whom everyone dumps undesirable work on. On the surface, it might seem that they're rewarded for being the ever-flexible one—"Oh, that Sarah, you can always count on her to come through and pick up the slack!"—but you know what? You can't pay a mortgage with praise. Gratitude is great, but doing too many favors can lead to being taken for granted. Being too accommodating doesn't guarantee a promotion or raise for being a team player; more than likely, it just ensures future crappy assignments.

Of course, working within the team structure is hugely important; in almost any work environment you need to be able to play nicely with others in order to get your own projects to succeed. But if all of your hard work is always for the benefit of the team or someone else, you come off as inconsequential.

If she'd been my client, the first thing I'd have told her is that she had to internalize that she had the right to say no. She had to learn to pause and count to five before answering any request for help. Also, she needed to ask herself, "If I say yes, how will this help me? Is there more here for me besides fulfilling my visceral desire to please? If I say yes, can I be sure there is a quid pro quo?" Setting professional boundaries would actually help her in the long run, because it would show she was serious about her career and could prioritize her work above pleasing others. When someone asked her for something, Sarah needed to learn that it was OK to ask for something in return. (If she didn't know what to ask for right then, she could say "I'm going to remind you about this later so you can return the favor!" and then follow up when she found herself in need of something.) Finally, Sarah needed to stop apologizing if she couldn't accommodate someone else's request, and remember that she is entitled to boundaries; she should tell herself, "I am not solely responsible for other people's happiness or success."

Unfortunately, Sarah had been a doormat for too long. Eventually, her boss was unable to see her as a person with initiative and a spine. And she herself had a hard time visualizing herself as authoritative in an environment where she'd been passive for so long; she'd developed too many ingrained habits to give herself an assertiveness makeover and make her new identity stick. She realized that many colleagues had become very accustomed to taking advantage of her—and they were not embracing of her newly discovered backbone. Eventually, she found a position in another firm where she could set a precedent of being tactful, direct, and pleasant but strong.

I think being passive and doing favors for everyone else is really about a person's own desire to be validated. You want to feel important, indispensable, and to have a great reputation. But you often wind up feeling resentful, even if you don't admit it to yourself. What's more, you're not actually helping your office function if it can't function without you. So if you think you're overly accommodating, what I'd urge you to do is visualize yourself being more vocal about your boundaries. Remember that this will lead to more respect, not less.

Accommodation in the Marketplace

In business, just as in politics, we have to engage in give-and-take interactions every day. Sometimes, we have to accommodate the other side to maintain the partnerships we have with others. These professional relationships are often based upon an understanding that if you scratch their back, they'll scratch yours. When negotiating a deal, for example, one company might have to give up short-term financial gain in order to acquire a company that will turn a profit in the future.

But accommodating people you work with is only one aspect of accommodation in business. More important is accommodating the needs of the market, which is the only way to stay relevant and ahead of your competition.

Businesses need to continually reinvent themselves or prove that their brand is distinct and of value if they want to edge out competitors and remain in the black. The failure to accommodate the market is one of the top reasons why businesses and the products they offer become obsolete. This is true even for businesses that were once built upon a strong model and proven history of success. No matter what the business is, none can afford to fail to accommodate trends in the marketplace that dictate consumer behavior and therefore influence sales.

Many businesses believe that they can ride out such trends if they only ratchet up their visibility through advertising campaigns; offer special deals, discounts, or rebate programs; or simply employ new marketing strategies. However, the failure to change the products to match the needs of the customer often proves to be a disastrous mistake.

Consider, for example, that twenty years ago, the publishing industry may have thought that its products were not at the mercy of the rapidly changing pace of technology. After all, the printed word was consumed through physical, as opposed to virtual, platforms—it was thought by many that the touch, texture, and simple routine comfort of holding a newspaper, for instance, could not be replicated. Anyone who follows the industry, however, knows that print publishing is now scrambling to accommodate what has been happening under its nose for too long.

A quick read of the way two booksellers, Borders and Barnes & Noble, handled the changing landscape offers interesting insight into accommodation and its importance. Both chains made their mark as retailers that pioneered the megabookstore industry. While we might take this for granted now, these two stores built their success because their large inventory and floor space allowed them to offer what other smaller bookstores could not offer at the time—access to a wide variety of books in one physical location.

Borders enjoyed early success even from its modest beginnings as a single store in Ann Arbor, Michigan, that opened in 1971. At the height of its success, Borders operated over 1,200 locations across the country. But since 2006, Borders was not able to post a profit and in September 2011, Borders closed the last of its stores after filing for bankruptcy.

What happened? The economy has taken a toll on many businesses large and small in the last few years. But some have been able to navigate these turbulent times better than others. These companies saw change occurring in the marketplace and instead of fighting it, they chose to capitalize on it—even if that meant that accommodating such trends would bring about significant changes to their business structure.

Borders' rival, Barnes & Noble, was one that did not overlook, ignore, or stubbornly refuse to adapt to a new marketplace. With the advent of new technologies, media were increasingly becoming digitized. Brick-and-mortar stores like Borders (which also had a large inventory of CDs and DVDs) began to see a sharp decline in sales as people turned to more efficient ways to browse, purchase, and consume media content. One such technology, the ebook reader, was blamed for stealing away a large chunk of sales from the stores. Amazon's Kindle offered readers instantaneous access to thousands of titles—all of which could be stored on a single tablet. Companies such as Netflix and iTunes allowed the same advantage for music and DVDs.

Unlike Borders, Barnes & Noble quickly realized that it had to adjust its business practices if it wanted to survive in this new and emerging digital environment. Borders clung to its roots and invested in revamping its brick-and-mortar stores and opening stores abroad. It also outsourced its online book sales to Amazon. Barnes & Noble, on the other hand, embraced the wave of the future and came out with the Nook—an ebook reader—and its own ebook site. The company also worked with the platform that was already there—the large amount of retail space it occupied—and focused on creating community environments with free Wi-Fi, Starbucks, and "Nook boutiques." Such boutiques consist of one-thousand-square-foot store displays where customers can learn about and try out the Nook. William J. Lynch, CEO of Barnes & Noble, has stated, "No other company is doing what Barnes & Noble is doing, utilizing its store footprint and innovative technology to add value to the customer's eReading experience—including unique features such as digital eBook lending, free Wi-Fi connectivity, in-store browsing of complete eBooks and exclusive content, and more."

Barnes & Noble no doubt has an uphill battle when facing competitors such as Apple's iPad and Amazon's Kindle, but so far it has managed to stay afloat in an increasingly digitalized world while still offering a unique community experience where customers can read, lounge, study, and socialize at one of the many physical locations found throughout the country. In August of 2011, just as Borders was preparing to close the doors of the few remaining stores that were still open, Barnes & Noble announced that digital content sales fueled mainly by ebook downloads had quadrupled in the past year. Sales of physical goods through its website increased by 37 percent, to almost $200 million.

Where Borders stubbornly continued to cling to a business model that was becoming obsolete, Barnes & Noble reinvented itself. Where Borders focused on pushing its product while failing to accommodate the customer's needs, Barnes & Noble leveraged technological advances to deliver that same product in ways that were well received. While Borders was inflexible when faced with the changes in how people were using and consuming media, Barnes & Noble altered its original business plan and identified partnerships that complemented this new strategy. In short, where Borders did not accommodate the changing marketplace, Barnes & Noble did.

Accommodation and the Yes-Men

Even if your need and desire to accommodate is more or less in balance, it can still be challenging when others around you don't have it quite so together in that regard and demand that you accommodate them. When we rely on or engage in close relationships with people who have a tendency to operate at the extreme end of this personality attribute, we risk being drawn into a preventable personal crisis. It's especially important to know you can get sucked into someone's need to be accommodated if that person has a lot of power or charisma—you may not even realize it's happening. People in positions of power such as celebrities, CEOs, and professional athletes represent a group whose members have a tendency to surround themselves with accommodating personalities—yes-men and -women—who will bend over backward to give the powerful person what he or she wants.

Unfortunately, what he or she wants is often not what he or she needs. There's no shortage of examples of this in the celebrity world, where we hear of doctors prescribing whatever a star requests, handlers cleaning up the wreckage of hotel rooms after a night of marauding, even parents of stars who are on the payroll accommodating their children's obvious substance abuse problems.

Indeed, there are many reasons a celebrity hits rock bottom—addiction, ego, fragile self-esteem—but a big one is being surrounded by overly accommodating people, or demanding that those around him accommodate, even if they normally wouldn't have that tendency. Why didn't anyone close to him or her say something? After all, if it were a friend or another loved one in our life who was rapidly approaching a crisis brought on by addiction, mental illness, or other destructive behavior, we would, hopefully, intervene.

In June of 2009, Michael Jackson died after overdosing on the powerful drug propofol. Propofol is rarely administered outside a hospital setting, yet Jackson's personal physician Dr. Conrad Murray regularly prescribed this potent anesthetic to help Jackson sleep. Jackson allegedly had a history of drug abuse and a host of other destructive behaviors but was known to beg doctors to prescribe him drugs to deal with his anxiety, insomnia, and pain. It was widely reported that Dr. Murray was promised payment to the tune of $150,000 a month for his services. Perhaps he thought that denying Jackson medication would be seen as a betrayal, or perhaps he was more concerned about the paycheck. Many in the Michael Jackson camp did not push the issue of his problems, perhaps out of a fear that they might alienate Michael.

Dr. Murray was charged in connection with Michael Jackson's death (and was found guilty of involuntary manslaughter), but Jackson was surrounded by people who should have been able to see how much pain he was in. According to Jackson biographer Ian Halperin, an aide close to the singer said this: "He is surrounded by enablers . . . We should be stopping him before he kills himself, but we just sit by and watch him medicate himself into oblivion." People in his inner circle let him live in a reality of his own making. Perhaps if those people had been less willing to go along with his every whim, the singer's story might have gone differently.

Another example of the over-accommodation of a celebrity's addiction is Anna Nicole Smith. Smith was the buxom blonde who rose to fame in the nineties as a popular *Playboy* playmate and Guess jeans model. Unfortunately, as her career began to decline, Smith became remembered more for disastrous public appearances and her reality show where she often seemed disoriented and confused. It became apparent to most spectators that she was often high, but it wasn't until after her death in 2007 that the public learned the true extent of the problem. In the hotel room where she died from a lethal combination of pain medication, sleeping pills, antianxiety medication, and various other drugs, authorities found several prescriptions that were not prescribed to Smith, but to her manager, lawyer, lover Howard K. Stern. The medication was legally prescribed by her doctor and friend, Khristine Eroshevich. Both Stern and Eroshevich were later tried, along with Dr. Sandeep Kapoor, for conspiring to furnish controlled substances and obtaining fraudulent prescriptions. Kapoor was acquitted, and the convictions of Stern, and the felony convictions of Eroshevich, were eventually set aside by the court for lack of evidence.

Larry Seidlin, the judge who presided over Anna Nicole Smith's body custody hearing, said this about Stern in a book he wrote about Smith's death (perhaps making a moral point rather than a legal one): "I think enablers should be punished . . . How about keeping her off drugs while she was alive? He was with her every day; how about saying no, and if she kicks your ass out, then goodbye and good luck."

That's something to keep in mind if you find yourself being asked to be a yes-person, either to someone powerful and charismatic or someone in your family: No one can completely control anyone's behavior, and when you confront addicts, they may indeed push you out of their lives completely, but that's a risk worth taking. It is clear that those who did remain close to these stars did little to help them recover from their addictions. Many went so far as enabling their addictions. Why do people become over-accommodators and behave this way when so much is at stake?

Over-accommodators may have many motives—not wanting to be cut off financially or emotionally, not knowing how to help, needing the addicted person to make them feel useful, or figuring that as bad off as the person is, he or she is better with their help than without it. But their behaviors basically boil down to not having enough courage to simply say no. Don't fall into that same trap yourself. If you're being asked to accommodate something that you know is hurtful to someone else, it's better to draw a line than to toe it. You may or may not be able to help the person you care about by urging him to get help, but you certainly are not helping by not saying anything. Sometimes the truth hurts, but in the long run it can save you and others from an avoidable crisis. And even if it doesn't, at least you will know you did everything you could.

Getting Back into Balance

So how do you know if, during a conflict, you should accommodate or place your wants and needs first? Conflict researchers Kenneth Thomas and Ralph Kilmann offer several concrete questions that you can ask yourself when you are faced with a potential conflict situation.

- Is supporting the needs of the other party feasible and appropriate, and will it not result in significant personal cost?
- Is preserving or building the relationship more important than winning the issue at hand?
- Is a negative outcome likely and is it better to end the dispute and move on?

If the answer is yes to these, then accommodation might be a healthy tactic to employ. It's healthy to accommodate when otherwise there is likely to be a negative outcome or an otherwise functional relationship will be severely damaged. But you also have to consider long-term versus shorter-term outcomes when navigating along the accommodation spectrum.

Applying the POWER Model

Let's apply the POWER model to the issue of accommodation:

Pinpoint the core trait: In this case, accommodation.
Own it: Acknowledge that it can be both good and bad.
Work it through: Process the role it's played in your life.
Explore it: Consider how it could play out in the future.
Rein it in: Establish how to reachieve balance and control.

PINPOINT the trait, which is in this case accommodation.

OWN IT: When you own the trait of accommodation, you acknowledge that it can be both a positive and negative attribute. It helps you get along and get things done as part of a team, but it can also encourage you to put your needs behind others in a way that is harmful to you.

WORK IT THROUGH: How do you recognize if you're an unaccommodating boss, spouse, or friend? First, notice if there's never any dissent at meetings or at the dinner table unless it comes from you. If you've cowed everyone, they won't want to stand up to you, which is a strong sign you're unaccommodating. At work, if you're experiencing a huge amount of turnover, that too is a warning bell. If you're constantly negotiating or finagling to get family and friends to do what you think they should, you'd best start monitoring and evaluating your actions. Controlling behavior can backfire, and while you will be accommodated for a time, no one likes to be ruled. For those who accommodate too much, find role models and mentors to assist you in assertiveness training. Counseling can also help you rediscover (or discover for the first time) the relief of putting your own priorities before others' when it's appropriate.

EXPLORE IT: Explore the issue by thinking about how your life might work out if you were less subordinate to the needs of others (if you over-accommodate). Acknowledge that you are not serving your own needs or those of your colleagues or family by being a pushover. If you are not accommodating enough, think about what it would be like to feel as though you have a partner or a team behind you—that's one of the benefits of accommodating others; it makes them want to accommodate you, rather than you having to push them to.

REIN IT IN: If you overly accommodate, make a conscious effort to make one change every day. Say no to a request to work late; refuse to cook if you're exhausted; turn down a plea for you to volunteer when you know it would be inconvenient. "Because I just can't," is a perfectly acceptable answer. If you're not accommodating enough, insist on putting the other person or people first, over their protests. If you're habitually someone who doesn't make room for others' needs, it may take a while for others to understand that you're trying to make a change. They'll catch on—and appreciate your efforts. Remember, a manageable, crisis-free life is predicated on knowing when to say no and when to say yes.

6.

PATIENCE

KNOWING WHEN TO HOLD 'EM
AND WHEN TO FOLD 'EM

My friend was a very good journalist who was noted for his fea-
ture stories, almost always appearing on the front page of the
newspaper. He was as thorough as he was eloquent—most of the
time. Recently, having received a tip about the birth of a child
to a flight attendant and a married high-ranking foreign dig-
nitary, he rushed his usual investigative process to scoop other
media outlets. He expected to get a lot of personal attention
and maybe even some television appearances once his story broke
and, in fact, he did. But he received even more attention when
a DNA test showed that the dignitary, who had denied any en-
counter with the woman, was actually not the father. Now he
was seeking my advice on some damage control, especially since a
lawsuit against the paper was a strong possibility.

I thought it uncharacteristic of him to be shoddy with his
reporting. He admitted he should've dug deeper but he wanted
to get the scoop. The newspaper he worked for was close to folding
and he was hoping this would help find him another job if indeed

the paper did go under. His impatience had gotten the better of him and now he was paying the price.

————

The words "Patience is a virtue" are uttered by everyone from the parent trying to teach her kid to wait his turn, to an apologist for the status quo, stonewalling a justifiably frustrated person who has been waiting too long for things to change. This highlights how this "virtue" can be hijacked for good or ill, and how while some patience is in fact a good thing, too much is not. As Kenny Rogers put it, "You have to know when to hold 'em, and know when to fold 'em."

Patience is defined as the capacity to accept or tolerate delay, trouble, or suffering without reacting in an inappropriate manner. Being patient means not quitting at the first sign that things are going to take awhile, which they often do. But you have to make sure that you're not just banging your head against the same wall; when you've tried every new solution that you can think of and feel yourself either repeating the same steps over and over again or simply getting furious, you've crossed the line between being patient and being stuck.

Patience is difficult for many of us because it seemingly requires us to simply stand by passively and not do anything (which isn't usually true—more on that later). It requires us to be acutely aware of the present moment; accept it, even if it's uncomfortable; and stay in it for an indefinite amount of time. Patience is antithetical to the lifestyles we live today. We're used to getting what we need pretty much right away. Our worlds are designed to hurry us through the present task we are engaging in and quickly move on to the next. We have express lanes, next-day shipping, express flights, and on-demand movies. Information that we once had to wait for, we now have instantaneous access to—we can bypass the delay with smart phones, the Internet, and email. Very little time is spent cultivating patience; instead, we try to find ways to make things even faster.

In Buddhism, however, patience is considered one of the perfections. Instead of being a passive process it is considered more of a "concentrated strength," as the British novelist and politician Edward G. Bulwer-Lytton put it. Patience requires practice, but it is believed that if one can master it, one will be a better person. In the book *Commit to Sit: Tools for Cultivating a Meditation Practice from the Pages of* Tricycle, Michele McDonald writes: "In Buddhism patience has three essential aspects: gentle forbearance, calm endurance of hardship, and acceptance of the truth." Because the human brain is hardwired for immediate rewards, being patient can be challenging.

On the other hand, being too patient, which some people are in the habit of, smacks of passive acceptance of something that may be unacceptable, and as with accommodation, having too much patience means you may be seen (or worse, feel like) a pushover. The "appropriate" reaction to something that is unjust, hurtful to others, or plain old wrong, is not patience but *im*patience, which often forces action on the part of those in a position to orchestrate change. Too much patience when you or others are being emotionally or physically worn down can be just as dangerous as not enough patience. Being told to be patient by someone who is in a position of power over you—whether it's your boss stalling on a raise, or a spouse who is asking you to forgo your needs for his—is often just another way of being told to suck it up.

Clearly, knowing when being patient is your best strategy, and knowing when to draw a line and say you're not waiting another minute, is critical both in achieving your goals and preventing a crisis. The key to mastering patience, however, is focusing on the implications of taking action now as opposed to waiting and seeing if any action is needed later. Finding the balance is not only about having too much or too little of this trait; it is also about deciding the optimal time to move forward.

As with the other traits we've discussed in this book, patience is something you have to moderate. Are you too patient or not patient enough? This chapter's aim is to help you be aware of the role patience plays in your life and psyche, so you can make sure it has worked and continues to work well for you. As with every other trait, there's a golden mean.

The True Virtue of Patience

Whether we like it or not, we need to practice some degree of patience in everyday life in order to coexist with others in society. When we pull up to a stop sign, we must wait for other cars to stop whizzing by before we can safely proceed across the intersection. If we don't, we risk causing a serious traffic incident. When we are in line at the coffee shop, we must wait for our turn despite the fact that the people in front of us are having difficulty choosing between the infinite varieties of caffeinated beverages offered—we can't just push them aside (no matter how much we want to) and demand that the barista fill our order first. On the flip side, if we are already running late, we might decide that waiting for coffee is not worth being late for an important meeting—our impatience with the coffee line results in a practical decision not to exercise our patience and be on time instead. We might honk our horns at the people not driving when a light turns green rather than patiently wait for them to notice it, which is of limited practical value. We make decisions every day that determine whether we employ patience or simply remove ourselves from the situation entirely and proceed to another course of action.

First let's look at the upside of patience, at how being able to moderate your impulse control can lead to success in life, work, and relationships. Too often, in today's hurried world, we want and expect instant results; even our computers, which offer time savings unheard of thirty years ago, seem as though they are taking too long if they go over thirty seconds to boot up. Thirty seconds, of course, is nothing if you're waiting for the customer in front of you to pay for his coffee—five minutes would more likely provoke your ire—and so patience is relative. Patience can be a difficult quality to exhibit if for no other reason than the anxiety of waiting that accompanies it. What if we wait and still don't get what we need? That time will be wasted. What if we wait and are late for something else? What if we wait and miss the boat entirely?

Yet the benefits of patience are often tangible; slow and

steady often truly does win the race. Think of the conscientious and diligent employee who learns the ranks as he rises in them and is trusted and relied upon for his experience within the company, as opposed to the corner-cutting whiz kid who is promoted beyond his ability and is at a loss when the crisis hits. Patience can lead to greater success or fulfillment by allowing us time to prepare and devise an appropriate strategy, which can ultimately lead to a greater reward.

Psychologist Walter Mischel began a series of studies in the 1960s looking at how kids dealt with the notion of delayed gratification—a future-oriented idea that means putting off a reward now to yield a potentially greater one later. His work became known as "the marshmallow test." Kids were given a marshmallow and a choice: They could have the one marshmallow now, or they could wait and then have two marshmallows later. Some kids immediately gobbled the marshmallow. Others tried to hold out for the second marshmallow, sitting alone in the empty room with the solitary sweet taunting them. Some turned their back on the marshmallow as a way to avoid temptation. Some covered their eyes. Some licked the marshmallow but didn't actually eat it.

When Mischel's team followed up on the kids over a decade later, the ones who were able to delay gratification and wait for the two-marshmallow reward had more social success in life, were more honest, had stronger relationships, and had achieved more academic success than the immediate eaters. It turns out that being able to resist eating a marshmallow that's staring you in the face (literally and metaphorically speaking) is a great way to predict success later in life. This and countless real-world examples speak to the value of cultivating patience if it's not your strong suit.

What's Behind Impatience

The longer I work with people in crisis, the more often I see other issues that masquerade as simple patience and impatience. We all have inside of us a childish "I want it now!" side that we've learned over time to temper (or at least most of us have, although there are certainly some demanding divas who have not). We lose patience when faced with discomfort in not getting our needs met. Our options then are to pitch a fit (that's the guy leaning on his horn or cutting the line) or to quit or shut down altogether and do nothing, a silent protest. The key to making thoughtful decisions about how to proceed when our sense of patience is being challenged (either by making us want to act prematurely or waiting too long) is to know what's behind your impatience or too much patience.

1. Impatience and Unrealistic Expectations

Sometimes, what appears to be simple impatience is really being disappointed by unrealistic expectations. You've no doubt heard the term "managing expectations." What that means is making sure people's expectations are in line with what they're liable to get, so they're not disappointed. Having unrealistic expectations will almost always lead to impatience. We see that in all aspects of business and life. Let's say that there's a flight delay, and the passengers have been strapped into their seats for two hours waiting for the plane to take off. They are getting antsy and impatient and rightly so: They paid for a ticket on a flight that was supposed to leave two hours earlier. If the flight crew says nothing or announces that "We'll be in the air in no time, folks!" and then the plane sits for another hour, the passengers are bound to be frustrated and impatient. But if the announcement explains what the trouble is, and gives a realistic estimate of when the plane will leave the ground, the passengers might be annoyed, but can recalibrate their expectations so their hopes are better aligned with reality.

The way our society views weight and getting into shape is another example of where expectations are often out of touch with reality, and leads to impatience—one of the top reasons why over 95 percent of all diets fail. We are led to believe through various media that dropping pounds is something that can be done quickly and effectively if we just try hard enough. The reality show *The Biggest Loser,* where contestants drop ten, even twenty pounds in one week, implies that rapid results are not only possible but commonplace. We search for the latest fads and are drawn to products claiming to trim our waistline in thirty days or less. Yet time after time we find ourselves after attempts to diet with ever more weight to lose. While there are many factors that go into weight loss and healthy living, one of the hardest things for people to accept is that any real lifestyle change takes time: time to break bad habits and time to form new healthy ones.

Karen, for example, has struggled with her weight most of her life. Her approach over the years has been to become concerned periodically, then try whatever popular fad diet is around. She's tried the chocolate diet (my favorite), the no-carbs diet, a "cleanse" diet, and many more. She would have varying success with them but once she lost the weight, she'd grow impatient with the diet and go off it. It wasn't long before she regained whatever she lost and sometimes even more. Eventually, Karen concluded that what she needed was not an intensive, impossible-to-sustain quick fix; she realized that if she wanted to get lasting results, it was necessary to change her eating habits permanently and begin to exercise regularly. It's a much slower process and requires more patience, but in the long run it's proving to be more effective. Although her results might not be as dramatic as what we've seen on TV, she has lost fifteen pounds and is still losing. If her expectations had been more aligned with reality—that change takes time—she might have come to that conclusion years earlier and saved herself lots of frustration and money spent on clothing she soon couldn't wear.

Karen used the POWER model. She was able to *pinpoint* her lack of patience in dealing with her weight loss—she saw that was the problem, not a failure of will or any individual diet. She began to *own* the fact that she had to accept that her impatience was preventing her from achieving her goals, that while impatience can work for you in some cases, this instance required patience. She began to *work through* her mental block by acknowledging how her lack of patience and rush to try "quick fix" fad diets had led her to become frustrated and give up in the past. She had to acknowledge that she often gained even more weight back. Karen chose to *explore* what she would do when she would inevitably encounter impatience in the future as she dieted. She enlisted the help of friends. She tracked her progress so she could clearly see the downward trend and she only weighed herself once a week. She finally had to *rein it in*: She began to develop more realistic goals. She focused not just on weight loss but on the benefits of healthy living, such as more stamina and overall feelings of well-being.

2. Impatience and Lack of Commitment

Some of us need to see immediate results in order to stay interested in a project, and that may be in part about not being that committed to the project in the first place. There's no crime in that—if something is not that important to you, perhaps a better route than looking for a quick fix would be to be honest with yourself that you're not committed, and work on something that you are committed to. If you feel you "should" be committed to something (exercise, for instance, or graduate school) but you're honestly not, you're not going to have the motivation to stick with it. This will look like impatience, but it's not exactly the same. Consider the experiment by Gary McPherson, the head of the Conservatorium of Music at the University of Melbourne in Australia. He studied 157 randomly selected kids as they chose and learned a musical instrument. Some of the kids quit, as kids do, and some went on to become excellent musicians.

What was the best predictor of success? Not talent or rhythm, not sensitivity, not household income or IQ. The single best predictor was the answer the kids gave to a question they were asked before they even chose their instruments: How long do you think you'll play? The kids who said, "Not long," quickly gave up; they didn't imagine themselves making the commitment to the instrument and so never incorporated playing into their goals. The kids who said, "A few years," had moderate success but for the most part did not stick with it. But the kids who said they were going to play for their entire lives were the ones who did the best by far.

As author and *New York Times* columnist David Brooks put it in *The Social Animal,* "The sense of identity that children brought to the first lesson was the spark that would set off all the improvement that would subsequently happen. It was a vision of their future self." The kids who were able to visualize themselves as musicians—who were committed to that end result—had a goal to work for, and they dedicated themselves to achieving that goal. They were ambitious and driven to succeed, and because they could picture the end goal they were willing to do the work it took to get there and not get impatient when they didn't become virtuosos overnight. Patience and determination are inextricably connected. If you're willing to do the work, you'll reap the results. Those who didn't perhaps simply weren't that invested in the first place, and so had no reason to be patient.

That doesn't mean that if you're simply committed enough to an outcome your patience will be unlimited and you can be successful in whatever you try, but it does help. Being honest with yourself about your true commitment to a project, and reevaluating your goals if you become impatient with the process, is a perfectly acceptable thing to do, and can save you a lot of wasted energy. Committing to something, growing impatient and then cutting corners, as we saw in the Denial chapter with the young author who plagiarized, can lead to major crisis.

Steve, an executive at an international sales company, is a great example of someone who made a realistic assessment of his level of commitment, and in so doing was able to work to the limit of his patience, with great results. Steve was one of those people to whom everything came easily. He was handsome, charming, athletic, and smart. But his job required a ton of travel to other countries, and one thing he was not good at was learning foreign languages. He realized, though, that being able to speak other languages was critical to his ability to succeed with his work. So he buckled down, took a course in German, since he traveled to Germany most, listened to language CDs in the car, and studied while he was on the road. Some of his colleagues laughed at the way he mangled the language, but he kept with it. Eventually he learned to speak passable German. It impressed the journalists and public relations people he interacted with in Germany, and he felt it was absolutely worth the resolve it had required of him. He told me, "I'm prouder of sticking with those language classes than I am of my sales figures or my house. Because sales is fun, and having a killer house is fun, but studying German wasn't fun. I wanted so badly to give up, and I didn't, and that makes my accomplishment a million times greater." He saw the value of his own patience, both professionally and psychologically.

At the same time, Steve wisely recognized that there were limits to his patience. In his work he traveled to France and Japan, so he started to take a French class and planned to take Japanese. He wound up dropping the class and opting instead to learn just a few phrases of each. Why? Because he wasn't as deeply committed. He saw that he did not have time for the amount of work or tenacity he'd need to learn two more languages, and realized that his doggedness wasn't infinite. He prioritized; he picked a goal and stuck with it, but he saw the point at which the rewards for his hard work would start to diminish. He could have viewed it as not having enough patience to learn those other languages; instead, he rightly saw it as a lack of commitment to learning those, given other ways he could spend his time and energy. It saved him a lot of frustration.

In this case, just as the POWER model suggests, Steve owned the trait and processed how patience could be good (helping him learn a language he'd use frequently) and how it could be negative (trying to have the patience to learn three languages at the same time might prevent him from ever mastering one). He weighed the options and happily chose his path.

3. Impatience and Impulsivity

Part of being patient is controlling one's impulses, and learning to do that is critical to building the skill set you need to really excel on both the personal and professional fronts. If you're a parent, you know that having children is one long test of patience (and if you've ever been on an airplane next to someone else's children, you know it can test your own patience). Parenting requires constant self-awareness and seemingly endless patience. Emma, a parent of two, knew that all too well. When one of her young sons had a tantrum or pushed limits, she tended to react quickly: to grab him and shush him (which often resulted in more screaming) or to give in to his demands, which of course sent the message that if he screamed, he'd get his way. The screaming, understandably, made her impatient for silence.

After a year or so of being shocked at how out of control her sons were, a friend clued her in to her pattern of reacting impulsively, and told her what worked with her sons when they were young: Stop, check her impulse to act fast to silence the kid, take a few deep breaths, and think. She discovered that she was more effective when she didn't react instantly, when she took a few moments to think about her parenting goal. Then she was able to target her response most effectively. Her natural inclination, like that of many people, was to respond to provocation instantly—anything to quiet her son, whose screams so jangled her nerves. But what's expedient is not always the wisest course of action in the long run, because it was only fixing the problem momentarily, not getting at the root cause.

The hardest thing in the world can be to hunker down when you want to be a blur of action. Yet we've certainly seen from the histories of celebrities and politicians in crisis that going off half-cocked is the stupidest thing you can do. Responding to a problem with screaming or lying, deflecting, stammering a poorly thought-out self-justifying semi-explanation . . . all those things will only hurt you in the long run. Not taking the time to come up with a fully thought-out response requires more, not less, damage control. It's far better to gather your thoughts, consider the impact of your words and behavior (what you've done already and what you have yet to do) on your loved ones and career, and then formulate a response. Even if that means questions and rumors and snarky comments are flying, you'd do better to sit with them, and sit with the discomfort. Knee-jerk behavior is not smart.

Once again, to employ the lingo of Philip Zimbardo that we discussed in previous chapters, we're talking the need to balance a present-time orientation and a future-time orientation. Often our responses to crises are designed to make us feel better as quickly as possible. But when we feel bad, our first response tends to be, "Quick! How do I feel less bad? Let me do that!" But what you really want is to be strategic in the long term.

4. Impatience and the Desire for More

Impatience can certainly serve as a counterweight to overanalysis, obsessiveness, and dithering. But it can also lead to lousy decision-making—especially when quick success makes us lust for more of the same. For example, Ken made a ton of money in a high-tech start-up early in his career. He was suddenly flush with cash at the age of twenty-six, and possibly because he hadn't had to be patient to achieve success, impulsivity ruled the day. He went off the rails in a manic spending spree, starting and acquiring new companies and buying houses, cars, and Jet Skis in rapid succession. He seemed to buy a new toy every five minutes, each purchase showing less judgment than the purchase before it. He'd made so much money so quickly that he was high on the feeling and impatient to feel it as intensely—on the hedonic treadmill we talked about in the Ambition chapter—and needed to buy more in order to feel the same level of satisfaction with his accomplishments.

In any case, he skipped due diligence: He didn't stop to think about business models, earnings projections, and the existing landscape for companies like the ones he was acquiring. All of these things required patience he simply didn't have access to right then. It was about being in the moment for him, trusting his gut in the here and now, rather than taking the time to accurately assess an opportunity. Examining details would curb the excitement for him and slow down the process he thought would be so successful.

His lack of patience hurt more than his business. Because he wasn't keeping track of where the money was going and he wasn't keeping his business manager informed, he found himself in trouble with the IRS. Things got more complicated when Ken sued the business manager for negligence and fraud, blaming him for his financial troubles. The manager countersued, saying he'd warned Ken that his prodigal lifestyle and penchant for acquiring new companies would sink him, and adding that he'd urged Ken to stop spending and think about the future. But Ken had no patience for that kind of long-term planning. He had no patience with his companies; he wanted them making money instantly. He'd be enamored with a new employee or new friend, then tire of them like a petulant child with a broken toy.

Rumors of bankruptcy began to emerge and they had to be controlled before it affected what was left of his businesses. I advised Ken to quickly settle with his business manager to take the dispute out of the public eye. I suggested a new accountant for him and that he allow the accountant more control over his finances. After that I suggested he try to counter the bankruptcy rumors by lining up some new opportunities and meetings for himself and then leaking that information to the press. He was eventually able to avoid bankruptcy by gaining an investor's support. He agreed to a budget and a system of checks and balances to curb his impulsive spending. On the personal front, Ken got counseling to put him in touch with what drove his rashness. Thus far he seems to be doing well and has cut back on his previous excessiveness.

Ken is a dramatic, multimillion-dollar example, but we all have friends who live beyond their means because they lack impulse control, which is of course a form of impatience. We've had colleagues who expect raises and perks before they've earned them and then either quit or become bitter when they don't receive them immediately. Being ambitious and motivated to succeed is a good thing, but the desire for more can inflame impatience. I always tell my clients, "Don't charge ahead before you know the lay of the land." You can't have an accurate assessment of the landscape if you're racing through it at a breakneck pace, and you won't make lasting alliances if you don't spend enough time at one job to meet people and develop relationships and alliances—all that takes time. A little bit of patience can give you all the tools you need to really understand—and understand how to succeed in—your environment.

5. Impatience and Autopilot

Sometimes, we become so accustomed to doing routine tasks that we skip steps and take shortcuts. We feel this is being more efficient rather than impatient—there might be some risk involved in doing so, but we figure that the quickest job done is the best job done. But situations in which you are so comfortable doing what you're doing that you go on autopilot can actually be costly. Consider when you first learned to drive. Remember how you took the time to adjust the mirrors, consciously check your surroundings, fully stop at stop signs, and actually slow down if the light turned yellow before you approached an intersection?

Now think about how you probably drive today; much of that has become second nature, so you don't need to take the time to really examine each thing—you already know how to do it. But when you are in a rush, running late or worried about getting lost, your mental process speeds up and you start getting reckless. Not double-checking to make sure your mirrors are perfectly adjusted because you know they're where you left them last time is fine; not checking your mirror to see if there's a car before you change lanes is a shortcut that is simply too dangerous to take. Unfortunately, the road is full of drivers like this—we lack patience. Because driving is such a routine activity we are more often on autopilot than we are engaged with what we are presently doing. If we were to all just slow down on the road figuratively and literally, perhaps hundreds of accidents could be prevented each day.

Impatience due to being on autopilot can be deadly in a hospital setting. Physician and *New Yorker* writer Atul Gawande wrote a book called *The Checklist Manifesto: How to Get Things Right* that looked at how ticking essential elements and activities off a list, even though doing so may seem silly, can prevent fatal errors. Everyone in a hospital knows what procedures you're supposed to follow to prevent infections at catheter sites. But in 2001, a critical-care physician at Johns Hopkins Hospital named Peter Pronovost decided to see what would happen if he created a checklist for those steps. They were laughably basic: Hospital staff should (1) always wash hands and use soap; (2) always clean the insertion site with antiseptic; (3) always put sterile drapes over the patient's entire body; (4) always wear a sterile mask, gown, gloves, and hat; and (5) always put a sterile dressing over the catheter site once the line is in. If you've ever watched *Grey's Anatomy,* you know all of these.

But Pronovost asked the ICU nurses to humor him and watch the hospital's doctors for a month to see whether they skipped any steps. Shockingly, they skipped at least one step with over one-third of the ICU's patients. Pronovost then gave nurses the authority to stop doctors if they saw them skip a step on the list. Enforcing the use of the checklist was essentially a way to enforce patience and care. After a year, the results were revolutionary: The infection rate plummeted from

11 percent to zero. Shocked, Pronovost and his colleagues decided to keep the experiment going for an additional fifteen months. In that entire time period there were two infections. The researchers calculated that using the checklist had prevented forty-three infections and eight deaths and had saved the hospital $2 million. The simple act of institutionalizing patience and making it part of the culture saved millions of dollars and eight lives.

Just as following checklists of seemingly obvious steps makes a big difference in hospital outcomes, so too does following a seemingly obvious checklist in your own life to make sure that your decisions are based as much on reason as they are on instinct. Just because something has become routine, don't forget or underestimate the consequences of inattention and proper follow-through; just as nurses had to be given the authority from above to block doctors from doing something negligent, there should be people in your life whose advice you listen to even if you don't like what you're hearing. Being able to hear, "Stop being impatient; put on the brakes; listen to what I have to say," could help us in romance, friendship, familial relationships, and work. It could also prevent small problems from blowing up into big crises.

6. Impatience and Corporate Responsibility
It's one thing to rush into a personal decision that affects oneself and one's family; however, for corporations to rush decisions that affect the safety of potentially thousands or even

millions of individuals is exponentially more dangerous. The crisis faced by Merck, the company that produced the drug Vioxx, is one with many valuable lessons on patience embedded within.

Before any drug hits the market, the Food and Drug Administration grants its stamp of approval. The public takes this to mean that the drug is safe and effective, and usually that's true. But many say that the evaluation process is flawed and that when so much money is at stake—it costs millions to develop the drug and do the testing the agency needs to give it its OK—and competition is so fierce, drug companies sometimes take shortcuts or engage in deceptive behaviors that hide incomplete data or exaggerate the effects of a potential drug. In other words, when impatience to get the drug to market overrides an approval process that, while flawed, is designed to ensure that a product is safe, judgment sometimes gets clouded and consumer safety takes a backseat to the maximization of profit.

In 1999, the FDA approved the pain reliever Vioxx, which was promoted as a better option than other nonsteroidal anti-inflammatory drugs (NSAIDS) such as aspirin, because of its lower risks of causing ulcers. Vioxx was positioned in direct competition with the drug Celebrex, which was developed by rival pharmaceutical giant Pfizer. Merck announced that its drug was more effective and could be used for a wider range of issues, and according to industry analysts, Merck had high expectations for how well Vioxx would sell.

In fact, its success was critical to the company. This was

because Merck's patents on several of its more popular drugs would soon expire, meaning other companies were free to develop generic (and cheaper) versions of the medications, thus eating into Merck's profits. Merck was on a tight timeline to make sure Vioxx was out in the markets as soon as possible or it would have to answer to shareholders. One analyst referred to Vioxx as Merck's "savior."

So important was this potential "savior" that corners were cut and eyes were closed, to the detriment of consumers and ultimately Merck. According to the *New York Times,* it was revealed that executives were made aware of possible safety concerns with Vioxx, but decided not to study the issue further to determine the true extent of the drug's side effects. They obviously needed this drug to work for them, and in this rush, they were all too willing to ignore the warning signs. (Notice how denial and groupthink played a role in this developing crisis: It's fine, no problem, just keep going.)

Initially, for them, their impatience paid off big—in 2003, Vioxx sales reached $2.5 billion and it was sold in eighty countries. It was one of Merck's best-selling drugs. Soon, however, reports of adverse side effects circulated in the public. In 2004, Merck voluntarily pulled Vioxx from the market amid safety concerns regarding possible adverse cardiovascular effects. It was too little too late: Studies from as early as 1999 and 2000, some believe, demonstrated the cardiovascular risk entailed in taking Vioxx, and emails between Merck executives also show that there was concern about the possible risks posed by the drug. A 2001 letter from the FDA called Merck's claims over Vioxx's safety "false and misleading." Merck claims that such evidence was taken out of context. They also claim that the company followed a "rigorous scientific process."

Yet by 2006, more than 9,650 lawsuits over Vioxx had been filed in state and federal courts. They allege that the drug was rushed to the market without the proper research demonstrating its safety. David Anstice, a former Merck executive, testified that the company was "under pressure" to push Vioxx out in the market. He said, "We were working very diligently and aggressively to get Vioxx to market as quickly as possible," in order not to lose market share to Celebrex.

The results of Merck's impatience are truly staggering. While the FDA said that 28,000 cardiovascular events occurred because of Vioxx, Dr. David Graham, in testimony before the Senate Finance Committee, raised those estimates and alleged that 88,000 to 139,000 people had suffered heart attacks or strokes as a result of taking Vioxx. As many as 40 percent who did, died. Graham added, "We are faced with what may be the single greatest drug safety catastrophe in the history of this country or the history of the world."

Merck reportedly won eleven out of sixteen suits at trial before agreeing to settle all claims. Merck paid the families of 3,468 users of its Vioxx painkiller who died of heart attacks or strokes. But there's nothing that can make up for the lives that were lost through impatience; the corporate crisis that the impatience led to is only about money, and this story illustrates that there are much greater losses that can be suffered if this trait is not kept in balance.

The Costs of Too Much Patience

There are times, however, when patience isn't such a virtue. If you keep on putting up with mistakes or duplicity, if you give not just second chances but third and fourth and fifth chances, what incentive does the other person have to change? Being patient can slip all too easily into being passive.

Think about the friend who keeps waiting for a promotion that never comes. You know he should change jobs; he'll never be seen as upper-management material where he is. He hasn't even been happy at work for months, but he's put in so much time that he feels certain his reward must be just around the corner. He's just sure that when this promotion happens, or when his boss is kicked upstairs, or when his office nemesis leaves, or when this particular horrible project after the last seventy-two horrible projects is over, then his work life will be fine.

Odds are, you know this isn't so. But he's determined to be patient, because he can't or won't see that he's the one who has to make a change. He can't or won't see that he's going to have to leave that job in order to have a happier work life. You know it; everyone knows it but him. In this case, there may be many other issues at work behind his "patience": He may be scared he won't find something better and afraid of the risks involved in leaving a sure thing; he may be afraid of change in general; or he may believe on some level that he is not worthy of a promotion, and to leave would only prove that. So he's "patient," endlessly so, and hides his fear and low self-esteem behind that virtue.

Or think about the friend who's been waiting for years

for her boyfriend to propose. They've been together for half a decade. She's determined to wait it out, thinking that when he gets over the rough patch at work, or at their next big anniversary, or when his mother gets over her diverticulitis, then he'll propose. But you can see that he's fine with things just as they are and has no reason to propose. You know she should cut bait, but she won't do it. In gambling, the promise of instant gratification can be a big draw, but when it doesn't happen right away, you start to feel as if you've invested too much to quit. The virtue of "patience" feels better than admitting you took a bad risk and are walking away with nothing. (Of course, investing more time likely means a bigger loss.)

We humans are great at talking ourselves into things we wish were true. In some ways, stasis is the easiest course. Telling yourself that you have a great plan and if you just wait a little longer you'll have the perfect opportunity to put that plan into action makes you feel in control of your destiny. But patience can turn into a rut too easily. The problem is that if you wait too long to put your plan into action, or if you wait too long for it to work once you finally do move ahead, you can convince yourself that you have control over a situation when you actually don't.

You might notice that this trait is somewhat linked to fear and denial. When is patience useful and when does it become a trait that holds you back? If you're trying to get what you want by coming at it from different angles, attempting new tactics, and remaining active in the process, that's okay. But patience without a backup plan and without action is simply wasted time. That is why the POWER model is especially useful when it comes to issues concerning patience.

Consider the out-of-work job seeker who patiently waits for potential employers to return his calls instead of taking the initiative to follow up himself. Maybe he is fearful that a decision has been made and he in fact didn't get the position. By delaying follow-up, he can at least continue to hold out hope. However, hope can keep him stuck and give him a reason not to move forward: He still has a shot at this job, so there's no need to come up with a backup plan yet. Or think about a woman trying to get pregnant. Patiently and diligently waiting for a miracle might not be the answer if there is a biological reason that she's having trouble, and having a plan of action (seeing a fertility specialist, perhaps) if things don't happen naturally after a reasonable time of trying is patience balanced with practicality. On the flip side, someone who has undergone several years of fertility treatment with no results may be in denial that she cannot biologically have her own children, and believe she's simply being patient. Costly treatments and failure to consider other options may limit her chances, in terms of both time and money, to consider surrogacy or adoption in the future.

In short, in any situation for which we are endlessly telling ourselves to be patient, we have to ask ourselves what our patience is giving us—we need to own it. Like the examples above, are we using patience so that we don't have to face our denial or our fears? Only then can we see if patience is serving as a virtue or a vice.

Just as having the right balance between patience and

impatience can help you avoid a crisis, once you're in one, the same tools can be helpful in digging out. Tony was the CEO of a Fortune 1000 company. The board viewed itself as patient and hands-off; it was a point of pride to the board members that they gave Tony the freedom he needed to do his job. This philosophy worked fine when the company was doing well.

But when the company began to flounder, the "we don't meddle" stance became a detriment to the company and then a strategic nightmare as they opted to patiently defer to Tony's direction and business sense—even though the company was slow to acquire other companies in an industry fueled by acquisitions and was quickly losing out on opportunities. Wall Street began losing faith that any turnaround would be forthcoming. But the board still refused to act. It was part of the board's collective identity: We have faith and we have patience that things will turn around. We hire great people and let them do their thing. Meanwhile, the value of the company was trickling away. The board's self-image as "patient" and "faithful" was actually harming the company. They were soon threatened with a shareholders' lawsuit. Eventually Tony, as well as some board members, had to resign.

What the board should have done to balance the freedom they gave Tony was to provide more oversight, advice, and guidance. The board has a responsibility to its shareholders to act in the best interest of the company, which is largely measured by profit. Perhaps, too, the board was in denial—a trait that, as mentioned above, often accompanies overly patient people. Perhaps they were fearful of what drastic action might signal to shareholders. Either way, their refusal to act caused a crisis that could have been avoided.

Waiting Out the Storm

At some point, we all find ourselves suffering the consequences of a bad situation that we have put ourselves in. While we wish that we could simply erase it from our record, we, of course, can't do that. Many of us wrongly choose to quickly sweep it under the rug in an impatient attempt to move on. But you've heard the expression "Haste makes waste"? We usually want to rush and to leave the difficulties that we've experienced in life behind us as quickly as possible, but that can make matters worse and lead to bigger problems. Every crisis has a fallout period, and the only way to recover from a crisis is to be mindful of the work that it is going to take to make that happen. If our actions negatively affected other people, they might not be prepared to move on as quickly as we are.

Furthermore, if we try to simply shake the discomfort without any insight into how we got to where we did, we are doomed to find ourselves in a similar situation in the future. A better approach to dealing with the consequences of our behavior is employing a form of active patience—recognizing that you might have to wait out the uncomfortable ramifications of a particular event in your life but developing a clear plan of action while you wait.

Actor Rob Lowe had a personal crisis in 1988 that he handled as well as possible, using the above strategy: waiting and using the time to develop a clear plan of action. You may recall that Lowe was a hot young Brat Packer whose career cratered when he starred in a homemade sex tape. The night before the Democratic National Convention in Atlanta, where Lowe had traveled to support Mike Dukakis, Lowe hit the bar scene with his pals Ally Sheedy and Judd Nelson. He picked up two women and took them back to his room at the Atlanta Hilton, where he filmed the resulting romp. Reportedly when Lowe was in the bathroom, the women left the hotel, along with the mini-cassette from their host's video camera and some of his money. The tape made its way to the publisher of *Screw* magazine. Al Goldstein aired it on his cable program. Copies of segments of the tape were later available for sale.

As if that wasn't humiliating enough, almost immediately the news broke that one of the Atlanta girls was only sixteen. Lowe instantly became an object of derision and disgust. Fortunately for him, the Fulton County DA chose not to prosecute him for recording himself having sex with a minor; he agreed to do twenty hours of community service.

Lowe handled his disgrace properly. He apologized for what he did (a real, satisfying apology) and then lay low for two years. He was patient rather than trying to crash back into people's good graces again too precipitously. He entered rehab—he acknowledged that he was an alcoholic and that he struggled with an addiction to painkillers in addition to showing some pretty lousy judgment. He used the disaster as an opportunity for self-assessment, and he showed humility instead of blaming others.

It couldn't have been easy to be patient and let the derisive press roll in and the gossip mill churn without responding.

But he did it. "There's no way that you could know how embarrassing it was," he told *People* magazine in 1990, when he started his comeback. "No matter what adjective I chose, it would be trivializing it." His friend Ally Sheedy told the magazine, "I just told him to duck and weather the storm and wait until his next work."

Sheedy's advice is good for all of us—when you're in crisis, sometimes you have to lie low and let your record speak for you. Being good at your job, focusing on the tasks at hand instead of your image, and winning back the trust of people closest to you are paramount in a crisis; whining about how you're being scapegoated or that your image is ruined endears you to no one. Lowe indicated that he was taking responsibility for his previous bad judgment and showed that he'd learned from his mistakes. "I learned that you must accept the consequences of your actions," he told *People*. "That's part of being the man I want to be."

He used the debacle as an opportunity to show that he was more than the callow, impulsive leading-man type he'd seemed to be. He patiently revamped his career; he stayed sober; he got married and, more importantly, stayed married. His patience paid off when he began to get dramatic roles he could really shine in—he gave a powerful, smart performance as Sam Seaborn on *The West Wing*, did good work in the nighttime drama *Brothers & Sisters* with Sally Field, and joined the cult hit *Parks and Recreation* doing straight-up comedy to great acclaim. In 2011, he published a memoir, *Stories I Only Tell My Friends*, to critical and commercial success.

Lowe's story is pretty much a model of how you stay

collected and patient during a crisis instead of panicking, responding dishonestly, or rushing to beg for redemption before people are willing to grant it. His crisis played out on the international stage, and his redemption took years to really take hold. As I write this, Lowe's redemption is so complete that pundits ask him to opine on the problems of his childhood friend Charlie Sheen. "Problem is, people go into rehab and they're not ready," he told CNN's Piers Morgan. "You want to get sober for your parents, you want to get sober for your job, you want to get sober for the cops, you want to get sober to protect your image . . . unfortunately, the only thing that works is that you have to want to get sober for you." Lowe's patience got him to where he wanted to be—thriving and flourishing with his career.

Applying the POWER Model

Pinpoint the core trait: In this case, patience.
Own it: Acknowledge that it can be both good and bad.
Work it through: Process the role it's played in your life.
Explore it: Consider how it could play out in the future.
Rein it in: Establish how to reachieve balance and control.

PINPOINT: The core trait we've pinpointed is patience.
OWN IT: When you own it, you embrace the fact that it can help you make better, smarter, more rewarding decisions about every facet of your life. You are also aware that without patience, you might be flying off half-cocked constantly; flitting from place to place without ever giving yourself a chance to really develop a skill; or indulging in constant, immediate

gratification, to your own detriment. But you also have to acknowledge that too much patience can make you hang on to outmoded dreams, refuse to see the world as it really is, and fail to take action when other people—be they employees or family members—are taking advantage of you.

WORK IT THROUGH: When you work through the role that patience has played in your life thus far, you have to consider whether you've kept the trait in balance. Do you tend to be too impatient, with unrealistic expectations of the universe and what it owes you, or do you err on the side of too much patience, experiencing some of the problems with passivity we talked about to a fuller degree in the Accommodation chapter?

EXPLORE IT: When you explore the way patience could affect your life in the future, you're really pondering how your life would play out if you showed more or less patience, whichever one you determined you needed in the previous step. How would your career be different? How much better equipped would you be to fulfill your dreams? What if you decided to ask a friend to tell you when you're giving others too much of the benefit of the doubt, being too patient with their flaws and failings?

REIN IT IN: When you rein it in, you find that the trait no longer brings imbalance to your life, work, and relationships. You'll discover that the proper point of equilibrium and control feels very good indeed.

7

INDULGENCE

KNOW WHEN TO SAY WHEN

She was this company's first ever female CEO. I knew of her and had always respected her intelligence as well as her toughness. She always seemed to have it together and was the kind of woman I would've loved to be mentored by when I was young. Right now, however, we were knocking heads, arguing. I was having a hard time getting her to cancel the annual lavish retreat the company had every year, always at a five-star resort in some fabulous location. The company had been doing it for years and she didn't want to be the first CEO to abandon tradition. Besides, everyone was eagerly anticipating the event. In part, she said, because it had been a particularly rough year for them. But this was exactly my point. They were asking for a partial bailout from the government and to continue with the planned retreat under such circumstances would be a PR nightmare—even if it didn't compare with the amounts of money needed to operate the company. Eventually, she gave in.

———

We work hard to pay for food, shelter, clothing, and health care. Those are necessities. But what we look forward to when those needs are met is spending whatever is left on things that bring us pleasure—and although it sometimes seems otherwise, a satellite dish, an iPad, and a long weekend someplace warm when the weather is gray are indulgences and not necessities. Indulgence is not always monetary. It is a treat in any form, a reward for our labors. For instance, we may try to eat healthy all week but allow ourselves one day during the weekend to eat whatever we want, whether it's good for us or not. It's the reward for our discipline, and as long as it doesn't threaten our goal of staying healthy, it can motivate us to stay on track.

What feels like an indulgence varies from person to person, depending on many elements such as values, culture, and individual preferences, but common to it all is that the indulgence is an exception to what we might have or do most of the time, and it universally brings us pleasure. It is usually something that would lose its specialness if we allowed ourselves to have it daily, or we would feel guilty about it, because there would be some unwanted effect if we did so (perhaps we would gain weight or siphon money away from a necessity or a more meaningful expenditure, such as a college savings plan for our children). Broadly, it is when we buy ourselves an expensive item, take time off, or engage in some activity or behavior that's not a necessity but a luxury.

Our country has profoundly mixed feelings about indulgence. On the one hand, our roots go back to the Puritans and the Protestant work ethic, which frowns upon indulgence in most any form. The reward for a job well done is having done that job well—not a 72-inch flat-screen TV. On the other extreme, we have the *Lifestyles of the Rich and Famous* mentality, in which we ogle and admire and judge the excesses of those who can afford it, simultaneously judging them and wishing we had what they had. Being part of American culture means having a somewhat schizophrenic outlook on reward and indulgence.

Indulgence in itself is neither good nor bad, although there is a such thing as healthy or unhealthy indulgence. We think of someone who is indulgent as sitting around watching TV and eating bonbons all day, but the desire to indulge, particularly as a reward for hard work, is healthy. As such, indulgence is a great motivator that may push us to make an extra effort at work—we feel that we have worked hard, or suffered greatly, or have gone so long without that we deserve to have or do what we want, purely for the pleasure of it. We are entitled to it because of our efforts or even our self-worth—e.g., "I'm a good person; I deserve to have this."

On the flip side, an indulgence-free existence is a grim one. If you only work-work-work, you burn out, and a life without the finer things—be it art, good food, the time to listen to music and relax with the people you love—would dry out the soul. If you don't expend any joyful capital here on earth, how will you spend it elsewhere? You can't take it with you, as the saying goes. If not now, when? We need both industry and play to have a fully rounded life.

One of my favorite examples of our split view of indulgence

is a founding father of this country, Benjamin Franklin. You might think Franklin came down squarely on the "be serious and abstemious" side. After all, he once wrote, "Early to bed and early to rise, makes a man healthy, wealthy and wise." Despite the seeming soberness of his quotation, though, Franklin was hardly the most puritanical guy in the colonies. He frequently indulged himself: He was known to love good music and good food, and he allegedly had many affairs despite being married. He knew the value of good work but recognized that there was much more to life and was aware of what was more seductive when he said, "There are more old drunkards than old doctors." It appears that our esteemed founding father worked hard and played hard.

To a certain extent, we are helpless in the face of indulgence. We appear to be programmed, evolutionarily speaking, to want what we want when we want it. Early humans didn't believe in delaying gratification. After all, back on the ancestral plain, most of human energy was devoted to finding and procuring enough calories to survive and reproduce, and no one knew whether there would be a tomorrow. Life was nasty, brutish, and short. A little indulgence of some kind—a few extra berries, a bear pelt, a roll in the tundra with a hot Neanderthal—was a pleasure that should be enjoyed in the moment because there was no telling just how much longer life would go on. We may in fact be programmed by the evolution of our genes to take advantage of what indulgences life offers us ASAP, even though we as modern beings can reasonably expect to be around tomorrow. The eat-dessert-first mentality can be hard to overcome. Food is a great example of how this instinct can lead to overindulgence: "We have evolved a predisposition to overconsume tasty food whenever it is available—and nowadays, tasty food is almost always available," Bradley Appelhans, now an assistant professor of Preventative Medicine at Rush Medical College, said in an article on Phoenix's AZCentral.com: "We are essentially hunter-gatherers in terms of our biology, and hunter-gatherers frequently had to endure lean times. . . . So we have evolved to be really good at storing fat. It's good for us. Well, it was good for us."

Combine the instinct to indulge when we have the opportunity with a drive for instant gratification and you can see why so many people have a problem with overdoing it. "Most physiological reward systems are measured with a stopwatch, not a calendar. With fight or flight, you know pronto whether running away was the right choice. Cocaine and gambling are now rewards," writes neurologist Robert Burton, in his book *On Being Certain: Believing You Are Right Even When You're Not*. "No one ever listened to the music of Bach with the goal of experiencing enjoyment in a month, or told a joke to make you laugh next year. Pleasure systems don't have a memory; they're now or never, measured within the time frame of synaptic transmission and neurotransmitter metabolism." Indulgences are about sensation, about the sudden rush of feeling. But those of us who are adept at delaying gratification at least somewhat enjoy the feeling of having something to look forward to, which is an indulgence in itself, albeit one that is less primal.

Of course, the advantages of not indulging ourselves to excess are clear. A quick look around you will provide ample evidence of the downside of overindulgence. As a society we struggle with obesity, debt, and underachievement. While there are mitigating forces that led us to those end points— you might find yourself in debt despite prudent saving and planning, and science has proven again and again that weight problems are not the result of a failure of willpower—overindulgence is at least partially responsible.

More dangerous still, in these days of instant access and abundance, indulgence without control can lead to addiction. As with all the traits that make up a human being, we want to find the appropriate balance in our lives. We need to indulge but we don't want to overindulge, whether in our own behavior or putting up with someone else's. And, although this is much rarer, we don't want to underindulge or not indulge at all.

In this chapter we will examine the pitfalls of various types of overindulgence and underindulgence and suggest how we might find a middle ground.

How Excessive Indulgence Can Lead to Crisis

As consumers of popular culture, we know that the dishiest stories are often ones about the rich and famous going off the rails on the indulgence train. While we may feel a pang of sorrow or empathy for those in crisis, especially if we've been through a crisis borne of overindulgence ourselves, we are far more likely to feel a sense of superiority and believe that we would be far better at controlling our tendency to overindulge if we were in their very expensive imported Italian shoes.

Maybe. Maybe not. It's hard to know how well we'd control our own temptations toward overindulgence if we were faced with the opportunity as often as the rich and famous. That's why looking at a few examples of the way overindulgence can spiral out of control can be helpful—the dramatic lessons we'll see in the coming examples contain principles that can be scaled back and extrapolated to apply to the everyday types of situations most of us face.

1. Overindulgence and Conspicuous Consumption

Hard work should be rewarded—I know no one who would disagree with that. To become a CEO of a major corporation, for example, requires ambition, intelligence, drive, passion, and determination. CEOs have to often sacrifice their time with family to get ahead in the boardroom. When others go home to sleep, they are still at the office. While their families enjoy vacations, they constantly have a cell phone to their ear. Most of us feel as though someone who works hard is entitled to enjoy the fruits of his labor.

But while nothing is wrong with spending your hard-earned money, more of those in power need to recognize that in a world where public perception can make or break you, the context and attitude with which you spend your money should be highly monitored. Flaunting your wealth when other people are suffering comes off as obnoxious—and often breeds resentment and judgment. Restricting expense accounts for client lunches but then booking the best resort for the executive committee's annual meeting is a slap in the face to the rank-and-file workers, especially when your company is laying off people left and right. Whether you are a CEO of a multinational company or a manager of a small restaurant, if you are in a position of power, you need to be aware of how your indulgences, especially in lean times, can fuel anger, backlash, and disloyalty.

It's amazing how some people can operate within a bubble and be blind to how their behavior may be perceived as excessively indulgent by others. It would take a lot for anyone to seem as self-indulgent as some of America's CEOs and Wall Street honchos, over the last few years especially; they have suffered a major image crisis. Not much was done to repair this image when, during the financial crisis of 2008, executives of failing companies were rewarded with golden parachutes and the three CEOs in the auto industry who were seeking a bailout for their floundering companies flew to Washington in private planes. Many executives appear out of touch with the dire realities of what is going on with the rest of the world— a world that is increasingly convinced that those CEOs and Wall Street types are causing the huge disparity in wealth in our country in the first place.

This frustration came to a head in the summer of 2011, with the Occupy Wall Street movement. The protesters involved in the Occupy Wall Street movement were, no doubt, fueled by stories of excess as protesters struggled in their everyday lives to simply make ends meet.

One of the uglier examples of this kind of clueless over-indulgence is the case of Dennis Kozlowski. You may recall that he was the CEO of Tyco International, the man who was convicted in 2005 of crimes related to his getting $81 million in supposedly unauthorized bonus pay. He's now in jail in New York State.

The press luxuriated in the details of Kozlowski's excesses. He allegedly had Tyco pay for all kinds of furnishings for his multimillion-dollar Manhattan apartment and Boca Raton compound. We heard all about the $6,000 shower curtain, the $2,200 wastebasket, the $3,000 coat hangers, and the $445 pincushion shaped like a turtle, all charged to Tyco. Kozlowski supposedly bought $17 million in art for Tyco's New Hampshire office, but empty boxes were shipped to New Hampshire (to establish a paper trail) while the art mysteri-ously wound up on Kozlowski's walls on Fifth Avenue. Tyco allegedly paid half the $2 million cost of Kozlowski's second wife's fortieth-birthday party on the isle of Sardinia in 2000, where guests were treated to valets dressed as half-naked gladiators, waiters and waitresses wearing togas and fig-leaf crowns, a golden chariot, a huge fireworks show, a full-size ice sculpture of Michelangelo's David urinating Stolichnaya vodka, a birthday cake shaped like a nude woman with spar-klers poking out of her breasts, and a performance by Jimmy Buffett. Prosecutors argued that the bash was disguised as a shareholder meeting. On a video shown to jurors over the defense's objections, Kozlowski says to his guests that the party will demonstrate "a Tyco core competency: the ability to party hard."

In 2003, Kozlowski threw another bash, a bachelor party for his future son-in-law, Thomas Bruderman, a trader for Fidelity. This party was on a yacht and allegedly included bikini-clad strippers, waiters on Jet Skis, intimations of prostitution and drug use, and a dwarf for hire. After news broke of the party, a grand jury began investigating whether corporate money was used for illicit doings, and the Securities and Exchange Commission began investigating charges that Bruderman received gifts from clients hoping for Fidelity's business. Bruderman himself ultimately left Fidelity. In 2011, he reached a settlement with the SEC, without admitting wrongdoing.

Even when the chickens came home to roost, Dennis Kozlowski didn't appear terribly sorry about defrauding people, let alone contrite about his level of indulgence at others' expense. While awaiting the verdict on his 2007 appeal, he was interviewed by Morley Safer on *60 Minutes*. He told Safer, "I was a guy sitting in a courtroom making $100 million a year . . . I think a juror sitting there just would have to say, 'All that money? He must have done something wrong.' I think it's as simple as that."

No, in fact the jurors were weighing whether he broke the law. Americans don't hate rich people. They want to be rich. It's the American dream, the notion that anyone can achieve wealth and success if he works hard. Kozlowski's comment was not only untrue, but it did nothing to help him gain the goodwill that he desperately needed.

It's not just the CEO who falls victim to overindulgence under public scrutiny; anybody can make poor-judgment goofs on a smaller scale. If you've ever flirted just a bit too much with someone who isn't your spouse at a party (indulging in the attention of another), if you laugh as you boastfully charge another few bottles of wine at a company dinner with a client, if you dabble in illegal drugs in a public setting in a world of cell-phone cameras . . . well, you're engaged in the kind of decision-making when overindulging that can lead to a crisis.

My advice for my clients: No matter how much fun you're having and how insulated and comfortable you may feel at the moment you're overindulging at a party or wherever, never say anything you wouldn't want your spouse or boss to hear. Never write anything on Facebook you wouldn't want your mom to read. Never pose for a picture or allow yourself to be in a video you wouldn't want shown at your birthday party. Never spend someone else's money in a way you'd have a hard time justifying to your superior, your spouse, and the IRS. So often we think we're anonymous. But in a world of security cameras, blogs repeating overheard gossip, digital fingerprints, and Internet footprints that reveal traces of who went where and when in cyberspace, you can never, ever assume you're not leaving a bright trail behind you.

2. Overindulgence and Being Called to Account

Stuff—we need very little of it but many of us enjoy material things, and that's not a problem until for reasons of divorce or audit one is called to account for how much one owns. Again—not a problem, really, unless you got some of it in nefarious ways.

Look at Los Angeles Dodgers owner Frank McCourt and his wife, Jamie. In 2009, the two announced that they'd be divorcing and immediately began to tangle over the ownership of the team. Their fighting got increasingly contentious as the two disputed how their fortune should be split. The fact that California is a community-property state made the battle for assets that much more intense. Lurid details about the two's prior indulgences began to hit the press. Newspapers gleefully reported on the couple, in happier days, spending six figures on an astrologer and paying no taxes. They were also accused of funneling millions of dollars from the Dodgers organization into their own pockets. They supposedly spent millions on homes, private jets, vacations, clothing, and jewelry. Not all of the alleged indulgences were about spending on material goods: Frank accused Jamie of having an affair with her bodyguard/driver (which she denied).

Conspicuous consumption aside, what was emerging in the headlines was how the couple got what they consumed. The McCourts divided the team's assets into dozens of small holding companies and moved fees, loans, and payments from one entity to another. At the same time, they cut the team's budget by $30 million. "Frank supposedly used the Dodgers as his private piggy bank," Loyola Law School professor Dan Schechter told the *Los Angeles Times*. "So if you borrow money against the company and you drain the proceeds for your personal use, that may be a fraudulent transfer."

Baseball commissioner Bud Selig finally yanked both McCourts from decision-making roles and appointed a trustee to deal with the club. The team ended up filing for bankruptcy and Frank McCourt lost his fight to retain ownership—he finally agreed to sell the team after a highly publicized battle. Both McCourts, in their greed and desire for more and better things to fuel their lavish lifestyles, bankrupted themselves morally and trashed their own reputations as well as their former prized asset. They were like King Solomon threatening to cut the baby in half, only they actually cut the baby in half and both ended up losing. During a public event in November 2011, Frank McCourt spoke to reporters and apologized for putting fans through the ownership drama that had unfolded over the past few years. He has also denied the allegations of "looting" team revenue.

Whatever the McCourts may or may not have done, the lessons from their saga seem so obvious it hurts to write: unchecked ego, a lot of ambition, and indulgent behavior are a dangerous combination. You need to keep your priorities squarely in mind in any decision-making you do regarding how and how much to indulge. While you will likely never experience a high-profile divorce like the McCourts', there may well be a time where you are called into account for your indulgences—and as in the POWER model, you're going to have to "own" and "rein in" that behavior.

3. Overindulgence and Addiction

There's a biochemical process to pleasure: Our brains are wired to respond to things we find enjoyable with a release of dopamine, a certain brain chemical. It floods our brains when we experience scrumptious food, wonderful music, divine smells, goose-bump-raising touches. Dopamine release can also be triggered by drugs, alcohol, nicotine, and gambling. Anything we really want to do—from playing chess to snorting cocaine to running marathons—probably involves some kind of brain-mediated reward system. Our bodies aren't designed to consider what's good for us in the long haul, so resisting these pleasure-producing sensations can be very difficult.

There is no one theory that can answer why some people seem more susceptible to addiction than others, and most treatment specialists believe that the causes of addiction are multidimensional. Some speculate that addiction is genetic, having to do with a deficit of naturally produced dopamine. "It is only when these individuals abuse drugs and alcohol that they feel those pleasures because the drugs stimulate dopamine production, which in turn stimulates their few dopamine receptors with the result that these individuals begin to feel good," writes Ernest Noble, professor emeritus of psychiatry and biobehavioral sciences at UCLA, in an article entitled "Genetic Research and Addiction," published online by *Counselor* magazine, a publication for addiction professionals. "But there's a trap in that, because continued use of the drug causes you to become addicted."

Still others suggest that addiction has less of a biological or chemical cause and is more of a symptom of a deeper psychological issue, the reasoning being that people who have emotionally healthy lives don't need to turn to drugs in order to be happy and fulfilled, or that undiagnosed mental illness is behind much addiction, as people attempt to self-medicate. "Heroin, for instance, is remarkably effective at 'normalizing' people who suffer from delusions and hallucinations (mostly schizophrenics)," writes Michael Segell, a writer for MSNBC .com, in an article called "Big Mystery: What Causes Addiction?" He continues, "Cocaine can quickly lift a depression, or enable a person with attention-deficit disorder to become better organized and focused."

One theory as to why some people are more likely to lapse into addiction than others that I find particularly compelling goes back to what we discussed in the chapter on ambition, where we talked a bit about the ways different people perceive time and how that affects the choices we make. Philip Zimbardo, the Stanford researcher who did that research, refers to the "present-hedonistic" attitude, by which he means a desire to enjoy life in the present tense and avoid all things that cause pain. Present-hedonistic types are all about immediate gratification and short-term payoffs. They tend to avoid people and situations they find boring or tedious, or work that requires a lot of effort or maintenance.

Zimbardo quotes a study by scientists at the University of Vermont that found that addicts were significantly higher on the scale of present hedonism and significantly lower on future orientation than non-addicts. "Don't they know the long-term negative consequences associated with continued drug use?" Zimbardo asks rhetorically. "Sure they do, but that is a way-out then, and the high from drugs is a nearby now." Similarly, present-focused students are more likely to be late in handing in homework assignments and more likely to blow off classes and meetings with advisers. They're more likely to be late and more likely to drop out.

Because the negative consequences of addiction usually don't take root immediately, and because at first indulgence in potentially addictive behavior is fun, addiction can be insidious. Most people who get hooked on cigarettes, alcohol, or shopping know intellectually that for every moment of joy there's a likely future cost. But abstract knowledge and current decision-making in extremely present-oriented people can be worlds apart. If you'd told Robert Downey Jr. about the risks he was taking with his career during his *Less Than Zero* partying days, he would likely have grinned at you and snorted another line. Statistics don't seem personally relevant to someone completely present-focused. Downey wasn't making spreadsheets looking at the cost-benefit analysis of hanging out at the Viper Room.

A good example of self-indulgence and eventual addiction is former Washington, D.C., mayor Marion Barry. He served as D.C.'s mayor from 1979 to 1991. In 1990, he was videotaped smoking crack in a hotel room with a woman not his wife and arrested by the FBI on drug charges. He was sentenced to six months in jail.

Barry had been suffering from an addiction to drugs and alcohol as early as 1987; in the months before his arrest his staff had supposedly begun scheduling all of his events and meetings for late in the day, since he couldn't make it into the office in the mornings. He reportedly fell asleep at his desk a lot, and he was known to have problems with the Internal Revenue Service, traffic violations, and possible shady dealings with one of his ex-girlfriends (he awarded her a city contract from which he might have derived personal benefit).

The international media were ravenous for any detail about Barry's arrest. I understood their interest and fascination, of course. The story had everything: drugs, power, and women. And once again, the issue here goes back to knowing the landscape. Barry should have known that his appetites were out of control. He should have known that, as a public official, he was being watched. Barry was in an extremely privileged position that came with plenty of perks and benefits. But thanks to a combination of unchecked ego and overindulgence in vices of all sorts, he wasn't satisfied with what he had and lost sight of reasonable risk. And I'm sure the drugs themselves clouded his vision of reality.

Barry, though, is an example of how even though he screwed up, that doesn't have to be a career-ending crisis. A lot of people were shocked when Barry was indicted and shocked when he was reelected as mayor in 1995. Both events made sense. He was hugely popular with portions of the African-American community, particularly people from low-income households. They saw him as someone who was fighting for their interests. That led those people to be inclined to indulge him in his excesses—self-interest on the part of his constituents bred forgiveness or at least forbearance. Political analyst Doni Glover put it this way in a 2009 WBAL TV-11 NBC interview: "he is accessible, he is aware of the needs of the people . . . and he is still known as a champion for their causes." Furthermore, many in D.C. at that time felt that Barry, who is African American, was being unfairly targeted because of his race, and many may have identified with the perceived injustices he was facing.

In an emotional public statement after his arrest, Barry said that he would "begin to heal [his] body, mind and soul." As tears welled up in his eyes, he admitted that he had a substance-abuse problem for the first time publicly. "How I wish I could trade this hour!" he cried to a crowd of spectators and journalists during a press conference. He continued, "I've come face to face with my deepest human failures. I've had to look my human weaknesses straight in the eye." He entered rehab and eventually served six months for cocaine possession.

His soul baring, combined with seeking professional help and serving his time, played well with his supporters, and he maintained their support. He is currently a member of the D.C. City Council, and while not without his continuing controversies, all things considered, he has bounced back quite well. Still, better if he had not had to bounce back in the first place, and a closer eye on his addiction would have saved him and his supporters a lot of grief.

You may say, "That's nice, but I'm not an addict! This has nothing to do with me!" Of course not all present-oriented folks are addicts. But present-oriented folks—are you one of them?—are the ones who are more likely to become addicts, because they're more prone to crave instant gratification and short-term rewards without thinking through or weighing the long-term consequences. And that can be a problem for any of us.

For instance, are you the type to quickly get frustrated

and quit a hobby if it doesn't come easily to you? (Even after you've spent a good chunk of change on fly-fishing or golf equipment, running shoes, copper cookware?) Or if you're really good at something, how hard do you work to improve it? Maybe you're a good golfer, but do you practice your swing and strive to get better? How hard do you push yourself? As Zimbardo points out in *The Time Paradox,* "Talent, intelligence and ability are necessary for success, but they are not sufficient. Discipline, perseverance and a sense of personal efficacy are also required. Childhood prodigies of any kind, for instance, rarely become successes in adulthood unless they have the discipline to spend endless hours at their craft."

In other words, you have to put in the work, all the time. And this means delaying gratification and postponing indulgence, restricting it and using it only as a reward for a job well done—after the job is done. As Zimbardo puts it, "Becoming future-oriented involves turning away from comforts of present existence and instant pleasure, the youthful temptation to play all day. It directs us away from the certainties of the here and now, black and white, is or is not, to a world of imagined options, of probabilities, of if-thens."

Indulging Others' Indulgences

Perhaps you don't have an issue with overindulgence, but someone around you does. It's worthwhile to examine whether what you do feeds into others' tendency to overindulge, whether you over-accommodate them to the point where they have no incentive to rein in their tendencies. This can lead to crisis for them and by extension for you. Have you ever been guilty of giving someone too many chances? A ne'er-do-well relative, a cheating boyfriend, a seductive but selfish girlfriend, an employee who seems like a lovely person but just keeps screwing up? Are you indulging them because you're too conflict-averse to address the core problems with their behavior or work? Are you indulging them because it makes you feel better about yourself, as if you're a kind and noble person? You're actually not doing them or yourself any favors. If you're the boss and indulge an employee so she doesn't learn, her mistakes are, in effect, your mistakes. Of course you are not responsible for another person's behavior, but you can be a contributor to an environment that makes it hard for an overindulgent person to control himself.

The Rarity of Underindulgence
Of course, the flip side of overindulgence is that rare thing, failure to indulge at all—in a way, deprivation becomes a perverse form of indulgence. We've talked about how being constantly abstemious and self-denying can cost you joy in daily living. It's important to plan ahead, but it's also important to enjoy the here and now. Saving for a rainy day is important, but so is singing in the rain. All things should be in balance.

Taken to the extreme, the model of underindulgence is Hetty Green, a woman who was born in the 1830s and died in 1916. She was the first woman to gain real power on Wall Street, an investment whiz and multimillionaire of the Gilded Age whose business acumen was legendary. But so was her stinginess. She refused to turn on the heat or hot water. She reportedly had only one dress and instructed her maid to wash only the hem to save money on detergent. At the time of her own death Green had amassed a fortune of over $100 million (over a billion dollars in today's money), yet she lived in tiny apartments in Brooklyn and Hoboken and frequently had dirty hands because she didn't want to waste soap. She carried a bucket of oatmeal to her office (heating it up on the radiator) so she wouldn't have to spend money on restaurant meals. When her son, Ned, broke his leg, she didn't want to spend money on a doctor, so she delayed getting him treatment. At last she took him to a free clinic for the poor, but they were turned away. She then tried home remedies. In the end, the leg had to be amputated.

Clearly, Green's behavior has overtones of mental illness. Why would Green feel the need to deny herself basic comforts? Why did she put her son's life in danger and deny him the standard care for a problem that did not have to turn into a catastrophic medical event? It's hard to tell, but for whatever reason, she obviously took frugality to the extreme. For some, extreme self-denial could stem from guilt, a fear that "giving in" will result in a loss of control, or overly neurotic tendencies.

Those who suffer from restrictive eating disorders often exhibit these traits. They deny themselves basic nourishment in order to achieve what is in their minds a perfect body. Anorexia, however, is not solely about food or body image. The issues run much deeper—restriction is just the method through which deeper psychological issues are expressed. Just as those who indulge may be driven by narcissism and greed, those who refuse to let themselves indulge may be driven by certain traits as well.

The word anorexia is often thrown around, especially in a culture with an incessant need to monitor the physiques of its celebrities. But anorexia is a serious disorder that is difficult to address and treat. In fact, anorexia has the highest mortality rate of any mental disorder. Those suffering from the disease tend to exhibit personality traits such as low self-esteem, perfectionism, neuroticism, and unhealthy obsessions. Their disorder is highly wrapped up in their identity. For the anorexic mind, the denial of food becomes a coping mechanism: When life is spinning out of control, a person suffering from anorexia turns to what he or she can control—food. Obsessively counting calories, measuring out minuscule amounts of nourishment, and focusing on weight all help the person avoid and compartmentalize issues in his or her life. Allowing oneself to "cave in to" the "luxury" of food equates to weakness and failure. Anorexics believe that they are deserving only if they stick to a strict regimen of food restriction and weight control. Continuing down this destructive path is equated with personal victory and achievement. Pride is drawn from the fact that an anorexic can subsist on an arbitrarily determined number of calories or shrink down to a certain size. Even at dangerously low weights, anorexics have trouble seeing themselves as anything but overweight—this fuels their desire to restrict even more in order to achieve "perfection."

Anorexia is an extreme case of underindulging. A rational mind would not draw the conclusion that eating a piece of cake signals that one is worthless and not worthy of love. But to some extent, we all exhibit irrational behaviors based on these notions of giving too much power to an idea or event. We don't take a well-deserved day off because we believe that if we do, the world will fall apart—it makes us feel out of control to be away from the office. We don't treat ourselves to a manicure or expensive haircut—even once in a blue moon—because we are concerned that it appears vain or costs too much money (even though we are more than happy to allow our kids to spend the money on something they want). We try to create an illusion that we are cool, calm, and collected no matter what the situation because we fear losing control. Some argue that anorexia and addiction are both attempts to control one's surroundings, that the anorexic is "addicted" to the control her self-denial gives her.

It's rare, in general, to have a problem of underindulgence (anorexia affects one-half of 1 percent of the population; compare that to obesity, which affects over 30 percent of the population, for example). However, not enjoying life and getting gratification from depriving yourself because you are driven by shame, guilt, or a sense of responsibility to someone else can just as readily create a crisis as enjoying the pleasures of life to the extreme. Let's look at the POWER model to see how we can healthily balance this trait.

Applying the POWER Model

Pinpoint the core trait: In this case indulgence.
Own it: Acknowledge that it can be both good and bad.
Work it through: Process the role it's played in your life.

Explore it: Consider how it could play out in the future.
Rein it in: Establish how to reachieve balance and control.

PINPOINT: Let's pinpoint indulgence and ponder how to own it.

OWN IT: In owning it, consider that not indulging yourself at all can lead to resentment, loneliness, joylessness, and the tendency to overindulge when you finally, inevitably let yourself go. But consider, too, that indulging yourself too much is self-destructive. You may end up doing things that are illicit or illegal, making a fool of yourself, losing the things that really matter to you.

WORK IT THROUGH: Work this exercise through by debating, honestly, whether you've let yourself fall too far toward one extreme or the other. Are you isolating yourself at work or in your social life because you refuse to indulge in bonding social activities? Or are you spending money you should be saving, using drugs or alcohol or gossip to excess, trying to buy the love of other people (parents, children, lovers, friends) with material objects?

EXPLORE: Explore what it would feel like to live with discomfort rather than overindulge or underindulge to blot out the feelings or feel the illusion of having them under control. What would happen if you decided to think in a more far-reaching, charitable, giving sort of way than the way you have generally viewed the world so far? Seek to make authentic connections that aren't dulled by drink or flashy spending.

REIN IT IN: And finally, rein it in by taking small steps, right now, to be a little less, or a little more, indulgent depending on which way you're leaning. Do what you have to do to reverse the momentum. Talk to a therapist about substance abuse or a financial planner about thinking for the future. If you've been too stiff or withdrawn to indulge at all, pick up the phone or ask someone at work to go to lunch. There are so many ways to keep indulgence—a dearth or a surfeit—from becoming a full-fledged crisis.

APPENDIXES

APOLOGIES: LOVE MEANS ALWAYS HAVING TO SAY YOU'RE SORRY

I've been doing what I do for many years, and it never ceases to amaze me that the very personality traits that boost us into the stratosphere can bring us crashing back down just as fast. My goal with this book is to keep you aware and on top of these aspects of who you are, which are the seeds of your success, with an eye toward maintaining equilibrium in your life, so that these same traits don't send you spiraling out of control.

We all, however, slip up from time to time, or despite our vigilance, we may get pulled into bad situations. Sometimes a problem is small enough that you can nip it in the bud. Sometimes it's so big that you can't imagine a way around it. Sometimes our actions—either because of negligence or by accident—can cause pain to the people around us. And the one indispensable tool we all have at our disposal when we do err is the apology.

Maybe "tool" isn't the right word; that makes an apology sound mercenary. Apologies are not contrivances or instruments to get you what you want. I see apologies as a way of conveying that you truly understand that you made a mistake—

perhaps a big one—and that you sincerely regret the hurt you've caused. While they are absolutely necessary, an apology shouldn't be viewed as a means to an end. An apology is an end in and of itself—even if it doesn't help your public image or even change the opinion of the person or people you're apologizing to. Even if you're not forgiven, the apology is for you as much as it is for the other person. If you know you owe someone an apology, you should deliver it.

Apologies have everything to do with the seven traits we've discussed in this book. The ability to own your mistake rather than deflect it or attempt to blame others is not a weakness. It's indicative of having a healthy ego rather than an out-of-control one. It means facing exactly what you've done rather than turning away in denial or fear of your own darkest impulses. And it means finding the patience to ride out the consequences of your actions. A heartfelt apology is a way of showing that human relationships are more important to you than your own raw ambition, your own need to look good at all costs.

"I'm Sorry but" and "I'm Sorry If" Are Not As Good As "I'm Sorry"

When I am strategizing with a client who is looking to mop up a crisis, I start by interviewing him about what he wants to say. I want it to come from the heart—from *his* heart. If something comes across as a statement produced by an army of handlers, it won't achieve its goal of feeling sincere and authentic. I talk to the person for a long time about what he or she did, what the impact was on others, and what he or she wants to say to those who were hurt. If the person is not in touch with how his actions affected others—if he doesn't *really get it*—the apology won't land emotionally where it needs to.

Here's an example of a less-than-satisfying apology. Philip Baker, a dean at the University of Alberta's medical school in Canada, gave a speech at his school's graduation banquet in 2011 that turned out to have been plagiarized. It was taken from a 2010 graduation speech by Dr. Atul Gawande, a surgeon and writer, that was published in *The New Yorker*. According to the *Toronto Star*, some students recognized Gawande's memorable term "velluvial matrix" from the speech, a term Gawande had made up to illustrate in his speech the idea that medical students have lots of unfamiliar vocabulary to master. Memories suddenly triggered by the quirky, invented medical terminology, several students Googled the words "velluvial matrix" on their smart phones, found Gawande's speech, and began following along. "Velluvial matrix sounds like something you should know about, doesn't it?" Gawande asked. "And that's the problem. I will let you in on a little secret. You never stop wondering if there is a velluvial matrix you should know about."

Baker did not help his cause with his apology to the class of 2011. He published a letter saying he regretted his "lapse in judgment" and added, "The talk was intended for a private audience, nevertheless, my failure to attribute the source of my inspiration is a matter of the utmost regret."

You can see the problem: Baker sounded as if stealing

someone else's speech was okay because he was talking to a "private audience," implying that he didn't expect members of that private audience to go public with his plagiarism, that the problem lies with the leak and not the fact that he passed off someone else's work as his own. The idea that it was a "lapse in judgment" and not a conscious attempt to present another's words as one's own is absurd. Calling something "the source of my inspiration" sounds a lot better than "the speech I lifted word for word," but being inspired by something usually means taking the germ of an idea and then saying something new about it—and even then credit should be given for the original idea. That he phrased his apology in the passive voice shows he does not see himself as fully responsible. That what he did was "a matter of the utmost regret" doesn't quite have the heartfelt zing of "I regret what I did." Finally, Baker said, "I offered a sincere written apology to Dr. Gawande and subsequently spoke with him. He was flattered by my use of his text, took no offense, and readily accepted my apology." Gawande's forgiveness of Baker's transgression is all well and good but is beside the point—he still cheated his audience, and it is to them that he should be apologizing. I give that apology an F on all counts.

When I advise my own colleagues and crisis-management clients on what constitutes a good apology, I say this:

- Be decisive, clear, credible, and direct.
- Tailor your message beyond the elites, as broadly as possible.
- Little good comes from looking back longingly.

Baker was not clear and credible. He issued a legalistic, poorly tailored apology. And in blaming those who leaked the fact that he'd plagiarized rather than owning the sin itself, he looked back longingly at that incident and conveyed that he regretted being caught, not what he did. Of course he wished other people hadn't told on him—who wouldn't? But that makes him look worse and the point of an apology is to make someone look better.

Some people seem utterly incapable of apologizing, well or otherwise. I've lost track of how many apologies Kanye West has had to make, and they never satisfy anyone. Part of success, professional or personal, is being liked, and while West may be admired for his work, his comments have turned off many who would otherwise have been open to enjoying it. He did an interview with the *Today* show's Matt Lauer to address his post-Katrina slam of President Bush, which Bush had discussed in his memoir and with Lauer as having been a low point of his presidency. West spent most of the interview acting persecuted himself.

When Lauer asked West to watch a clip of an emotional President Bush responding to his accusations, West defensively retorted, "I didn't need you guys to show me a tape in order to, like, prompt my emotion to what I am going to say." (The purpose, of course, was to inform the viewership, but West couldn't imagine that. Instead, West took the airing of the video personally, as people with out-of-control egos are apt to do.)

Later in the interview, while West was expressing regret about what he said about President Bush, he claimed to understand Bush's anger because he, too, felt judged when people called his 2009 MTV awards comments about Taylor Swift racially motivated. (As discussed in Chapter 1, West interrupted Swift's award-acceptance speech, opining that Beyoncé should have won. Beyoncé is African American, as is West. Swift is white.) During the conversation, another clip rolled in the background, this time of his outburst on MTV. West, again, took issue with the video: "Yo, how am I supposed to talk if you're going to run this thing in the middle of while I'm talking?" He later turned to someone off camera and said, "Please don't let that happen again . . . it's, like, ridiculous." Lauer pointed out that there was nothing unusual about running the clip. He said, "It's something that we do every day, when a guest is talking about an incident or a location, we run video. . . ." West later tweeted a string of rants including: "Yo I really wonder if Matt Lauer thought that s*** was cool to play the 'MTV' clip while I was speaking about Bush?"

I'm afraid I wouldn't know what to say to West about how to apologize more effectively if he were my client. I think I'd advise him to try very hard to remember that he is there to address the fact that *other people* were offended, and that the moment needed to be about those people he hurt, and their feelings. He made the *Today* appearance about himself yet again—what he didn't like, how he wasn't getting to say whatever he wanted, the way he wanted. If West was unable to deliver an apology that didn't require an apology, perhaps he'd have been better off holding his tongue.

The Elements of an Apology

"An apology can't be an apology in name only and just because a declaration contains the word 'sorry' or 'regret' doesn't make it satisfying. In fact, a weak apology can make things worse," writes Marsha L. Wagner, the ombudsperson at Columbia University whose writing on mediation in university settings is cited by colleges all over the country. "An apology is a powerful means of reconciliation and restoring trust. However, sometimes even a well-intentioned apology can exacerbate a conflict." This gets back to our larger point about balance—when you think about what a real apology is supposed to say and do, you're less likely to spin your apology into something that creates even more scorched earth and damage.

Wagner says the essential elements of an apology include the following. (The elements are hers; the examples of how they work are mine.)

1. A common understanding of the exact substance and nature of the offense or perceived offense.
(For example, you could say, "When I made that comment about your work, I immediately knew it was a low blow," or " I realize I hurt you deeply when I betrayed your trust by reading your email.")

2. Recognition of responsibility or accountability on the part of the one who offended.
(For example, you could say, "Blaming my temper is no excuse for what I said," or "I promised I would do

something and I didn't do it—even if I told someone else to
do it for me, the responsibility is still mine.")

3. Acknowledgment of the pain or embarrassment that
the offended party experienced.
(For example, "If someone had said that to me, I would
have been totally mortified," or "I know what I did
will have huge repercussions in your office and in your
life.")

4. A judgment about the offense.
(For example, "What I did was wrong," or "What I said
was despicable." It's not good enough to say, "I know you
think what I did was wrong," or "It appears some people
felt what I said was despicable." That makes it seems as if
you do not agree that you acted badly, and opens the door
to the idea that the other person is too sensitive or otherwise
has some strange quirk that would lead him or her to be
offended by what you said or did.)

5. A statement of regret.
(For example, "I am so sorry I used that word in front of
your mother," or "I am regretful about my actions with the
pool boy.")

6. An indication of future intentions.
(For example, "I will never do anything like that again,"
or "I will work hard to make sure that you are not put in
that situation again.")

Be very careful to own every aspect of the behavior in explaining why you did what you did. As Wagner points out, you don't want to offer a defensive justification. In other words, it's fine to say, "I was trying to be funny, and the result was hurtful and stupid." It's not fine to say, "I should have known people don't have a sense of humor about this subject." It's fine to say, "I lost my temper"; it's not fine to say, "When I'm drunk I say things I don't mean."

I'd add this to Wagner's excellent rundown: Never blame others, even if you feel that whatever happened is not all your fault. That may be so, but this is your apology and your goal is to own what you did without spreading the blame around. If others had a role, hopefully that will come out, but this is about what you did; it's on you.

Golfer Tiger Woods's apology stands out in my mind. After his infidelities were discovered, he knew he'd let many people down—fans, sponsors, and of course his family. He needed to apologize, and it needed to be satisfying. Woods stood at a lectern in front of a blue velvet curtain, looking like a nervous high schooler about to deliver a report he'd just illegally downloaded from a term-paper site on the Internet. Some viewers found his awkwardness touching. Others found the entire scene too calculated. Sally Jenkins of the *Washington Post* wrote:

> Woods and his handlers staged a fake news conference
> to apologize for being fake. To these ears, it was stilted
> and rehearsed to the point of insincerity . . . The nature
> of the proceedings—the limiting of admission to a few

friends, the refusal to entertain any queries, even from a set of golf writers who have been egregiously kind to him—suggested that Woods is still determined to have things on his own terms. Which calls into question just how much he's changed, or whether he even thinks he needs to.

I disagree with that assessment. I understand why Woods did it the way he did—he doesn't do well in spontaneous interviews and he has real skittishness around the press. I think the actual content of Woods's speech was good. And I think that content is relevant to anyone who needs to make restitution for bad behavior. As I see it, here's what he did right:

- Woods took ownership and responsibility for his actions; he didn't try to pass the buck. That's what you need to do when you've let your ego get out of control.
- He apologized to the right people—in his case, his family, his fans, his sponsors, and the game of golf.
- He asked for forgiveness, reminded us that we are all human, and admitted he'd been seduced by his own fame and fortune.
- Just as importantly, he admitted his need for help. He addressed false rumors (in this case about domestic violence) directly. He made his boundaries clear, which in his case meant telling the media to stay away from his wife and children.

The Best Defense

Sometimes the offense is bad enough that even a well-crafted apology can't help. You may remember that comedian and voice-over actor Gilbert Gottfried (he was the voice of Iago in the *Aladdin* movie) tweeted a series of unfunny tsunami jokes within hours of the huge Japanese disaster in March 2011. They included, "My Japanese doctor advised me that to stay healthy I need 50 million gallons of water a day," and "I was talking to my Japanese real estate agent. I said, 'Is there a school in this area.' She said, 'Not now, but just wait.'" The tweets were met with horror. Gottfried responded, "I sincerely apologize to anyone who was offended by my attempt at humor regarding the tragedy in Japan. I meant no disrespect, and my thoughts are with the victims and their families." That was a perfectly fine apology, but he'd already gone too far. He lost his longtime job as the voice of the Aflac duck.

I do not know Gottfried and I can't speak to his motivation in making those jokes. A charitable interpretation is that, like many comedians, he was simply finding black humor in the horror that the universe sometimes dishes out. And in some situations, that kind of humor can relieve the tension people are feeling and unite folks in a bitter laugh about something awful, making everyone feel better. This was not one of those situations. Massive loss of human life is never funny, and even if you are inclined to black humor or humor that's in poor taste (and some people are), it was far too soon to be joking publicly when so many people were suffering. Perhaps it was Gottfried's ego getting the best of him, in believing anyone would want to hear what he had to say, or some misguided sense of ambition where he felt he needed to stay in the public eye for his career's sake. I don't know.

But his example provides a good lesson for the rest of us. The best apology is the one you don't have to make, because you used your powers of evaluation and balance in the personality traits we discussed in this book to avoid making a dumb mistake in the first place. I wish you every bit of good luck in going forward with your life and career, and may reading this book ensure that you never need the services of someone who does what I do.

THOUGHTS ON NAVIGATING A CRISIS

My goal with this book is helping you avoid the kind of crises that have kept me busy for the last twenty years. But just in case you've gotten hold of this book when you're already in the thick of a crisis, here's my list of things to bear in mind when the unthinkable happens. It's something I revisit after each case I work on. If I've learned something new about human nature or the nature of scandal after working on a case, I add it to the list. And you better believe I keep a copy in my desk drawer . . . always.

1. Trust your gut.
2. Know the facts—not what you *want* them to be, but what they *are*.
3. Never assume you know everything.
4. The truth always comes out—it's only a question of when.
5. Read the climate—know the landscape.
6. Know where you want to end up.
7. Know when to hold and when to fold.
8. Admit you are in trouble.
9. Don't overreact.
10. You will know when to walk away.
11. Things usually get worse before they get better.
12. Expect the unexpected.
13. Crises occur irrespective of one's fame, power, or prestige . . . so deal with it.

ACKNOWLEDGMENTS

The first person I must acknowledge is Chris Garrett: without him, this book would never have made it to publication. Thanks for your insight, your hard work, and your commitment to traveling this road with me. It has been quite a journey. It was conceived late one night in the office after strategizing on how to deal with a client's crisis. We started to think about all the crises we've dealt with and how many of them share the same core issues and traits. Any success I have is shared with you. And a special thanks to Stacey and Grant, Chris's family, for providing him with all the love, support, and room he needs to help me do what we do every day—crisis!

Thanks to the other members of the team who stuck with me through the late nights and early mornings. Kim Price—you are a lifesaver! I so appreciate the all-nighters, the early mornings, the many calls, and your invaluable insight—and special thanks for the times we reviewed the material at our favorite Mexican restaurant. And thank you Mona Horton, for your contributions and for always being just a phone call away. You are always there when I need you the most!

Thanks to the SWAT team of friends and family, who took the time to read the book and provided constructive feedback: Tina Lifford, VeTalle J. Fusilier, Darren Grubbs, Sally Travi, Fay Boulware, and Kristen McGhee.

Thanks to Dominick Anfuso and Leah Miller and the whole team at Simon & Schuster/Free Press. Leah, we did it! Thanks for hanging in there with me and for all the encouragement and support you gave to a first-time author who desperately needed it. Most of all, thanks for your friendship.

And to the team at Fletcher & Co.: Christy Fletcher and Rebecca Gradinger, thanks for your wisdom and making sure I did not write just another crisis book. Rebecca, thanks for being a superagent—taking all my late night calls and riding the roller coaster of a first-time author with me. You never gave up—thanks for keeping the faith!

Thanks to the folks who kept me going with their encouragement and support: Robin Marcus, who has been doing that for the last thirty years. Tina Lifford—I think we were separated at birth—loving you! Pat Lomax, blessed to have you as a friend. And Laura Branker—thanks for your friendship and for harassing me about making those deadlines.

Specials thanks and lots of love to the surrogates my parents left who have always looked after our family. Thanks to Ophelia Thomas, William "Punkin" Kilgore, Francine M. Graves, and Uncle George. Our parents left some wonderful angels to help us. Thanks for all your love and support.

ABOUT THE AUTHOR

In a career spanning nearly twenty-five years, **Judy Smith** has served as a crisis adviser to a host of famous clients. Her unique combination of communication skills, media savvy, and legal and political acumen has put her high in demand during some of the most high-profile events in recent history: the President Clinton scandal, the Iran Contra investigation, the prosecution of former D.C. mayor Marion Barry, the Supreme Court confirmation hearings of Justice Clarence Thomas, the Chandra Levy investigation, and the Enron Congressional inquiry, to name just a few. Smith has also provided strategic advice to Fortune 500 corporations on a variety of corporate communication issues as well as to leaders in nations including Haiti, Jamaica, the Turks and Caicos Islands, and the Kingdom of Saudi Arabia. Her expertise as a crisis manager serves as the basis and inspiration for the upcoming ABC television series *Scandal.*